EX LIBRIS

VINTAGE CLASSICS

ETHELIND FEARON

The Reluctant Hostess

ILLUSTRATED BY ALEX JARDINE

WITH AN INTRODUCTION BY KATIE FFORDE

VINTAGE BOOKS
London

Published by Vintage 2015

1

First published in 1954 by Herbert Jenkins Ltd
Copyright © Ethelind Fearon
Illustrations © Alex Jardine

Vintage
Random House, 20 Vauxhall Bridge Road,
London SW1V 2SA

www.vintage-classics.info

Addresses for companies within The Random House Group Limited
can be found at: www.randomhouse.co.uk/offices.htm

The Random House Group Limited Reg. No. 954009

A CIP catalogue record for this book is available from the British Library

ISBN 9781784870300

Printed and bound in Germany by

GGP Media GmbH, Pößneck

TO
JULIA CLEMENTS
who taught me how to do
the Flowers

CONTENTS

Introduction

I have always been an anxious – bordering on the hysterical – hostess. It's not that I don't want my friends to come and for me to feed them and make sure they have too much to drink – I do! But I always get in a bit of a panic first.

Before we had our house done up there was always a need to adjust the potted plants to hide a stain on the carpet or more importantly, catch the drips from the leaking conservatory. (In bad weather it was a water feature, illuminated by fairy lights.)

If I'd had this charming volume to hand I'd have done it all with less panic and a great deal more panache. This book gives you confidence, confidence that no matter what household disaster occurs five minutes before the guests are due, you can overcome them. And she tells you how. Not the pathetic 'darling could you possibly fix (the boiler, the front door, the roof) . . .' for her. With this book to hand you climb the step ladder and do it yourself.

But at least these days, people aren't obliged to entertain if they don't want to. I remember my parents (my father was desperately antisocial) having parties every year when we lived in London when I was little. The ice was bought in blocks from the fishmonger as we didn't have a fridge – what happened to it then I can't tell you as I don't know. It may have been put in the bath. Cocktails and sherry were served, as were crisps, which came in large blue and white striped boxes and were never seen at any other time.

The Reluctant Hostess by Ethelind Fearon takes us back to the days of enforced party giving. We can all picture the scene – random aunts, uncles and cousins, the neighbours, the boss, the secretary, all had to be invited (but possibly not the charlady.) Anyone who's read *One Pair of Hands* by Monica Dickens will recognise the people in this world even though that describes a much earlier era. Reading the book almost made me miss those more rigorous times.

Then, entertaining didn't mean bring a bottle, and bread and cheese in the kitchen. You had to put on a good show. There had to be cocktails, 'cups' and canapés, and not of simple bits of French stick covered with something bought from Waitrose. No, these involved aspic, works of art on crackers or toast so thin it seemed ironed, celery turned into boats, radishes into roses etc. (Although this is the counsel of perfection.)

There is also a section called Some Ghastly Games. These days we don't often play party games and although personally, I'd always be happy to (I secretly love Karaoke) no-one would think badly of you didn't include them.

However, if you do feel you'd like to add this layer read the instructions carefully. Do not go unprepared into this enterprise. We are told of parties where the hostess has had to provide 'soot, biscuits, a carving knife, two candlesticks and two night-dresses, a top hat, a pack of cards with each one cut into unequal halves, lipstick, a piece of coal, a walking-stick, a bowl of flour, 6 empty match-boxes and two empty beer bottles.' (This would mean proper night-dresses, not worn-out t-shirts with Hello Kitty on them.)

Given the title and general supportiveness of the book

one kind of hopes that Ethelind will go on to say how completely unnecessary all this is. But no! Such detailed preparations are essential. She says, (and however much one quails at the thought of having to find all those things as well as turning tomatoes into fairy toadstools with the aid of salad cream), 'Nothing is more macabre than a distracted hostess simulating a ghastly gaiety, with every game she ever played gone clean out of her head and a raging desire to burst into tears, take her shoes off, and be alone in the dark.' And no one could argue with that.

But take heart, she does have simpler games to suggest (as well as many complicated ones) and she encourages the hostess to allow guests to suggest favourite games. 'Parties are like pigs. You can't push them, only lead them, and if it will run itself, so much the better for everyone.'

This book is written for the inhabitants of the real world. No Martha Stewart or Nigella Lawson's perfection here. This is for women who have worn carpets, smoking chimneys and broken chair legs, multi skilled and resourceful.

Just as well, really, because these real people are expected to be perfect hostesses at all times. If guests turn up unexpectedly, you can't say, 'Lovely to see you, I haven't got a thing to eat, let's go to the pub.' No, you have to pretend you are ever ready for guests, and produce soup, a main course and pudding. Fortunately in those days there was more likely to be some sort of servant who could run out and buy some emergency ingredient, like a block of ice cream. (Yes, there is a recipe). Nowadays it would be the hostess who would be leaping in the car and dashing

XII THE RELUCTANT HOSTESS

out to the 8-til-Late. But in those days you had to be seen
to be producing guest-quality meals at all times.

And, as dear Ethelind says, (after reading her book I do
feel she's a friend,) 'Entertaining isn't just ordering a
gargantuan meal and then writing a proportionate cheque.
It is planning the most pleasure for the most people with
the least pain to yourself.'

Frankly, the 'least pain to yourself' bit would be best
served by ordering it all from Ocado and having it delivered,
but what you got for your money wouldn't be a proper
party or true hospitality. There needs to be a bit of personal
input. Then, and now. I would never suggest people distress
bought mince pies (why would anyone do that?) but there
has to be some personal contribution that will make the
party recognisably yours. I have a friend who dips those
soft ready-to-eat prunes in melted chocolate. They are
delicious and only she ever makes them.

Then, people weren't so gastronomically sophisticated.
You could give them Bovril and tinned veg and call it 'clear
soup.' And if you follow the directions and fill your store
cupboard as directed you can knock up the food for a small
wedding breakfast or a five course dinner party, possibly
both, without any extra virgin olive oil or harissa paste or
powdered sumac or any of the things we feel are essential
staples these days.

But what most endears me to this enchanting book is
the brio, the joire de vivre that our Reluctant Hostess brings
to the task. She gives it her absolutely best shot, she makes
her guests truly happy because she is so happy to see them.
Whatever domestic disaster may have occurred just before

she opens the front door, you know she will have a smile on her face and genuine welcome in her heart. I may well have to give a cocktail party myself, with proper canapés, with aspic.

I suggest that if up to now you've been a Reluctant Hostess, read this book and be Reluctant no more!

Katie Fforde, 2015

1

The Theory and Practice of Entertaining

IN the Stone Age people lived in their own caves, stalked their own food—a fair contest between man and beast with no holds barred—and ate it themselves, habits with much to recommend them. Entertaining began—like a lot of other customs—in the East.

There was a law—in a time so far back that they only made important ones and people could therefore remember them—that if you had eaten bread and salt with your neighbour you couldn't poison him during the current year. Or he couldn't poison *you*, I forget which. Probably a bit of both.

So people of good sense took care to dine out pretty often even if they *had* better food at home, because it wasn't so much a meal as an insurance policy.

About half-way between Them and Us came the Borgias,

who stepped round the insurance policy in an artful way by not serving salt at all, they used arsenic. After a few preliminary (or 'warming-up') courses, the two substances look pretty similar.

Thus they kept the rules and eliminated their enemies at one blow.

Nowadays people are not poisoned, they only *think* they are.

And for some psychological reason which is difficult to discover they still give and take parties pretty frequently while simultaneously grumbling about the necessity of so doing.

In this case it is more blessed to give than to receive, because in your own home you can control all (or most) of the elements of a party. They are predictable and when you *know* what is the worst that can happen and its probable duration, you can endure it with fortitude.

We will suppose then, that there is a group of people to whom you owe kindly words, a few drinks and some decorative, but not necessarily nourishing, food. People don't go to parties to be nourished. Most of them go out of curiosity, some for display, some because they have no valid alternative, and some because that evening is otherwise empty and a vacuum is the one thing they can't abide. But they will mostly come for one reason or the other, so you must first determine how to work off the largest number with the least trouble and then send out the invitations—and in this connection check the list several times for possible omissions. There is no sharper serpent than the overlooked guest to whom honour was due. She may decry the idea of parties, she may even genuinely dislike them, but by Heaven if she isn't present the echoes of this horrid oversight will reverberate round your head until party time comes again.

How should an invitation be sent?

Usually in the third person.

> *Mr and Mrs Periwinkle request the pleasure of Miss Plumtree's company on Friday the somethingth of something at 8.30.*
>
> *Dancing.*   *Canasta.*   *R.S.V.P.*

To which you reply in the same style addressing it to Mrs Periwinkle and declaring that 'Miss Plumtree has much pleasure, etc.' never '*will* have much pleasure'. And don't delay longer than a couple of days before answering. It is not considered nice manners to deliberate too long and in any case it's better to get the thing over quickly and not brood over it.

The more formal an invitation the longer before the event you must issue it. A month for dances, a fortnight for dinners or evening card-parties, a week for afternoon-parties, and even less for cocktails which are a cross between a cup final and a self-service counter.

As for the receiving end of all this, be as punctual as you can at dinners because of soufflés and such-like light-weight cookery whose constitutions may be delicate. But, even if you walk round the block seventeen times before daring to ring the bell, never *never* be too early. Composure drops like a mask upon the hostess at the last moment, but to catch her unmasked and in the chaos which normally reigns just prior to zero hour, is the unforgivable and unforgettable crime.

I recall the painful state of my friend Mrs Nabob who, in the half-hour before a clear-soup-cold-salmon-chicken-and-soufflé dinner, was reviewing the table and the situation and had a sudden thought about mayonnaise. She reached for it off the top shelf in the larder.

The jar was slippery and she caught it squarely on the top layer of curls.

But she is a woman of great ingenuity and after the panic and turmoil had subsided and she had been restored with aspirin and brandy, quickly washed her hair, called to the maid to make some Hollandaise and stuck her head in a large paper carrier to concentrate the heat from her hair dryer, which was of the 'pistol' type. Unfortunately her husband was using the electric plug in the bathroom for his shaver so she plugged in to the point in the drawing-room and when a subsequent ring at the door bell—unheard because of sauce-beating and hair-blowing—announced the premature arrival of Sir Digby and Lady Brown, who were

frightfully pukka, the small daughter of the house ushered them in upon a grisly scene.

Mrs Nabob, far from receiving guests, was pacing the floor in agitation and a bath-robe, with her head in a bag and apparently a revolver raised to her temple with intent to fire.

You can't laugh that off with ex-Poona people, and they still think that they saved her from a Ghastly End, even though five minutes later she was blown dry and in her right mind again.

There are two points worthy of note here. *Never come early to a party, you never know* WHAT *you may be interrupting.* And if you *do* put treacle or anything on your hair by mistake stick your head in a bag to dry it. It only takes a few minutes. A bucket would do as well, but is less comfortable, and if discovered looks even worse. You might also try keeping spillable liquids on a lower shelf.

You've got them at your dinner-party then, and your husband has managed his black tie. I will discuss table-laying later but just now we will consider menus.

Don't try to do too much. And don't have everything hot or you will be jumping up and down in the most upsetting way, worrying and sniffing for possible kitchen catastrophes like a terrier at a rat-hole.

Have your cocktails and snippets in the drawing-room first unless you prefer to start with soup and sherry at the table, and arrange one hot and one cold course alternately. For instance:

Lobster Bouchées (hot)   Roast Pheasants (hot)
Jellied soup (cold)   green salad
                                              Lemon soufflé (cold)

★   ★   ★

Cocktail snacks (cold)   Cold chicken and salad
Cream of tomato soup (hot)   Zabaglione (warm) with
                                            sponge fingers

* * *

Cheese bobs (hot)   Kidney flan (hot)
Cold salmon and salad   green salad
                               Orange meringue pie
                                  (cold)

* * *

Kipper snacks (hot)   Sole in cider (hot)
Scotch eggs and endive (cold) Chocolate soufflé (cold)

* * *

Cold jellied soup   Fruit set in jelly
Roast duck and orange   Caper fingers (hot)
   salad (hot)

and so on—trying to alternate not only the hot and the cold
but the light and the heavy.

A buffet supper is much less formal and less trouble.
Moreover you can invite two or three times the number
that you can possibly seat at a dining-table and they have
much more fun.

Push the big table back against the wall and arrange a
series of small tables to accommodate about four each. Or
failing tables let them sit haphazard round the room which
takes up even less space. After they have chosen plate,
implements and food at the buffet and got themselves sat
somewhere, you can circulate with drinks, either coffee or
alcoholic.

Food should be capable of being consumed with a fork and
there is an endless variety of delicious 'mingles' which can

be made hours before and either re-heated or kept hot or cold in large quantity: risotto or several flans of kidney; corned beef rabbit; cubed ham and tongue with salad (cold); chicken (cubed) and pineapple salad; fried chicken or fried turkey in thick gravy with noodles; cups of hot soup; chicken or rabbit gumbo; salmon or haddock pie; American fish pie; baked fish fillets rolled in bacon, served alongside baked beans and mashed potatoes (with cream, butter, and egg beaten into them); crab or lobster meat heated in good Hollandaise sauce, plus chopped hard-boiled egg, surrounded by a ring of fluffy potatoes as above; the same crab or lobster in a bath of mayonnaise and a ring of salad (cold); hamburgers and any form of sausages; spaghetti with cubes of meat and tomato purée.

Or you can prepare individual plates of cold food beforehand, one for each guest. A *candle salad* is a ring of pineapple with a peeled banana (dipped in lemon juice to prevent discolouration) stuck in the hole, surrounded by lettuce, mayonnaise and cubed ham, with radish 'fuchsias' for a garnish. It looks party-ish and tastes very festive too.

Pepper salad. A combination of chopped pineapple, chopped green pepper, and chopped tomato, mingled with cream cheese and mayonnaise and served either in soup cups or empty grapefruit skins is another winner.

And chicken (or rabbit) cubed and mixed with mayonnaise, chopped grapefruit flesh, shredded lettuce and cucumber, with small cubes of beetroot added at the last moment is delicious. But all these 'salad' things must be well seasoned or they are insipid.

The dessert which follows can be a cold soufflé, trifle, or other creamy sweet, or, if you have a large refrigerator, some concoction, amalgamation, or declension, of ice-cream. The great point is to keep it simple and have it—like the hot dishes for the buffet—made hours beforehand so that you don't have to worry at the last minute. Try chocolate ice-cream topped with chopped pineapple and glacé cherry; peaches on vanilla topped with whipped cream; hulled strawberries and cubed pineapple worked into vanilla ice and re-frozen; tinned apricots smothered in vanilla ice into which chopped nuts and cherries are worked; vanilla ice rolled in peanuts with a covering of chocolate sauce. All these can be prepared ready in their individual goblets and kept cold until needed, and there are many more in *Ice-Cream Dishes, How to Make Them*, by Gretel Beer.

An evening bridge-party can either rely on a buffet supper similar to this, or use sandwiches served at the tables with ice-cream to follow, but an afternoon bridge-party is merely an affair of small thin sandwiches, bridge rolls and tiny cakes such as you will find in my little book, *Fancy Cakes and Pastries*. Keep off the 'cut and come again' kind of cake—you aren't supposed to be *feeding* the people, only entertaining them.

Cocktail-parties are the best way of all to work off an enormous lot of people in a small space at very little cost. So long as they have two square feet of floor space per head they will survive. We don't worry about cubic air space. The more it is like the Black Hole of Calcutta the more they think they are enjoying themselves, but don't have the room too hot at first. They will all have come in from the chillier air outside, and to be catapulted suddenly into tropical heat can be very disturbing to the equilibrium.

It is a nuisance if this becomes so deranged as to assume the horizontal and much kinder to keep the heating low at first and let the mob warm it up gradually.

A party of this kind can easily be put on for half a crown a head if you make the stuff at home, as directed in the two following chapters, and the buffet table again comes into operation.

Have a husband, son, friend or other reliable male to stand behind it and dispense the drinks—vast jugs of which can be 'fixed' beforehand and left in the refrigerator. I don't advocate a professional barman because he will only make them in his own way which is always a more expensive one.

Most cocktail-shakers are hideously inadequate in size and I find that the largest decanter you can buy (or a large ornamental bottle with a close stopper) makes a much better 'shaker'. Directions for labelling glasses, making cocktail-snacks, and arranging the buffet follow in appropriate chapters, and it only remains to add that about two hours is long enough for a cocktail-party, whichever side of the counter you may be on.

So we come at last to the fatal moment, when there are no more days to tick off the calendar, the relentless face of the electric clock is grimacing the hour at you, and at the other side of the door, composing their faces into the proper shapes, lurk those who—for some reason which now eludes you—you have invited to take meat and drink at your abode.

It rather looks as if there's no retreat, doesn't it! Nothing can save you now, so we'd better get on with it.

Greet each guest as if his or her arrival was the one thing for which you have been waiting this long long while. See that they have shed all necessary portions of their clothing (and in the room dedicated to their use make sure there are the component parts of First Aid to Frocks—safety-pins, needles, cotton, clothes-brush and adhesive tape) and introduce them to those already there.

In the case of cocktail-parties you can't introduce everybody to *everybody*, you can only pick out the likely ones and throw them together hoping they'll stick. If they stick too closely tear them apart and split them up. Circulate well yourself and see that the others circulate too, and don't forget that in introducing them you introduce the gentleman to the lady never the other way round—no matter if he is marquis and she a plain miss. If she is too plain you may be sure that in due course he will introduce himself to someone more congenial.

Now let us explore the important question of food.

2

Cunning with Cocktail Accompaniments

I SUPPOSE if we're going to begin at the beginning we'd better see about fixing some cocktail snippets, those invariable preludes to a formal meal, which cost as much as the meal itself if you buy them in Piccadilly and absolutely nothing when you make them at home.

They are all so agreeably simple. Anything mangled up and sitting on a biscuit is a cocktail snippet.

If you want to learn the whole art of Cocktail Snacks read Mollie Stanley Wrench's little book on the subject. I only give you here what I have found to be the simplest and easiest and most foolproof selection. You can easily toss up a dozen varieties of them—sufficient for 25–30 guests, in one afternoon and I *know* because I've often done it.

The foundation of many cocktail snippets—the raft on which they sit, is a round or oblong cheese biscuit, about half the area of a small box of matches and quite thin, made thus:

3 oz. plain flour, 1½ oz. grated cheese, 1½ oz. butter or marg., salt, cayenne, yolk of an egg, and water to mix.

Rub fat into sifted flour, add cheese, plenty of salt and cayenne, egg yolk and *just* enough water to make it bind together stiffly. Too much water will make it hard. Roll and stamp out, some with a small cutter, about 1¼ inches across and 1¼ inch thick, cut others into oblongs, and bake fifteen minutes in a moderate oven or until firm and golden. When cold spread with one of the following mixtures:

Grated cheese and mayonnaise with a little finely chopped parsley.

Skinned and boned sardines mashed with lemon juice and a little butter.

Drained and soaked black olives, 4 drained and soaked anchovies, 2 oz. butter, a teaspoonful of parsley and a little dry thyme and bay leaf powdered. Pound all this with a good shake of pepper and a teaspoonful each of brandy and lemon juice.

Anchovies pounded with knob of butter.

Bloater ditto.

A layer of mayonnaise covered with a circle of raw pink ham.

A layer of savoury butter (mixed with bovril) and a circle of hard-boiled egg.

Some Cocktail Snippets

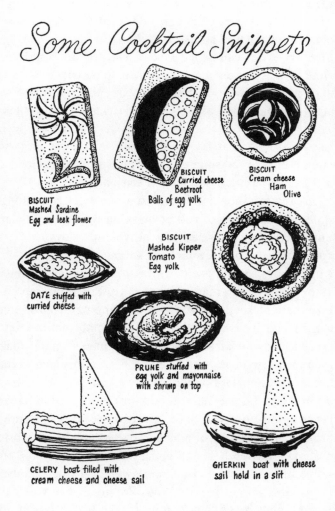

BISCUIT
Mashed Sardine
Egg and leek flower

BISCUIT
Curried cheese
Beetroot
Balls of egg yolk

BISCUIT
Cream cheese
Ham
Olive

BISCUIT
Mashed Kipper
Tomato
Egg yolk

DATE stuffed with
curried cheese

PRUNE stuffed with
egg yolk and mayonnaise
with shrimp on top

CELERY boat filled with
cream cheese and cheese sail

GHERKIN boat with cheese
sail held in a slit

Cooked kipper boned and pounded with butter.

Peas (if not green enough add a little green colour) pounded with butter and grated cheese.

On top of this can be put savoury stuff of any contrasting colour. What you use for bottoms on some can be tops on the others and they look best crowned with a small knob of yet a *third* colour—an asparagus tip, a square of tomato flesh, slice of stuffed olive, grain of caviar, caper, triangle of cheese, sprig of parsley, ball of egg yolk pounded with butter, a minute radish cut to the shape of a fuchsia and so on. But everything must be well seasoned.

This is a tradition and is said to provoke a thirst, though as the partakers thereof will be drinking *your* sherry I can't think why one should do any provoking. However, it is expected of us and therefore we submit.

If you wish to be *really* professional, having arranged a number of oblong masterpieces as per diagrams you may glaze them to keep the things from slipping off. You may even, if you have a steady hand, do small pictures on a dark background of sardine or Gentleman's relish, make a star or a moon in white egg, a flower in piped cream cheese with a bit of boiled leek for a leaf, a green boat of gerkin with a cheese sail (all laid flat) or on a white cream cheese or mayonnaise base lay a pink shrimp, a curled anchovy, a symphony of crab and capers or a bit of lobster coral and caviare. There is no end of variations and permutations and it is a game to which all the members of the family may be admitted. Provided that you have made enough bases they can each take half a dozen and have a competition as to the result; they can't hurt a thing and if they eat too many 'bases' you can always buy more from the grocer.

Having made your little pictures, lay all your biscuits side by side in a clean shallow tin and pour over them a clear glaze made like a jelly from:

Half teaspoonful Bovril in half gill of water and ¼ oz. of powdered gelatine. Wait until it is nearly setting, then spoon it lightly over them. When one layer has set give it another and subsequently a third and when cold cut them apart with a sharp-pointed knife.

I always do the oblongs in two dimensions and the rounds in three and I have been assured that the kipper twists and stuffed dates are in *four* because they are not of this world at all.

For these you take a strip of cheese pastry, finger size (I can see you'd better double the quantities for that cheese pastry) and a strip of raw kipper to match, the thick boneless part under the ribs—one fish will yield eight such strips. Anchor them together by a dab of raw egg and a bit of pinching at both ends, twist about three times and lay on a greased tin. When you have enough (although actually there are *never* enough, one could always do with more) cook them about fifteen minutes in a moderate oven and don't let anyone know about them until the party is ready to begin.

Curried dates are stuffed with a mixture of cream cheese, mayonnaise or sandwich spread, grated cheese or anything white that comes handy mashed with a little lemon juice and enough curry powder to be interesting but not enough to make the victim yell. And it is generally admitted to be a great improvement on Nature's idea of a stone.

Walnut kisses are good and original. Mash cream cheese with meat extract and cream and put between two half-walnuts. Let it protrude a little at one side and dip lightly in finely chopped parsley.

And *olive walnuts* are usually a surprise. Take a stuffed olive, roll it in cream cheese and then in chopped walnuts. Serve on a pick like its predecessor.

Stuffed prunes are soaked for twenty-four hours, then dried and stoned but not cooked, and filled with a squashed-pea and yoke-of-egg mixture, with a sprinkle of lobster coral or very pink shrimp where they gape open. Very subtle.

Salted almonds are the easiest thing on earth, you merely blanch your nuts, fry them golden brown in a saucepan with olive oil and shake in a little salt.

Cheese straws are easy too: 2 oz. each of grated cheese, plain flour, fine breadcrumbs and butter, with salt, pepper, and cayenne. Rub fat into flour, add cheese and crumbs, and mix to a stiff ball with as little water as will hold it together. Roll out ¼ inch thick, cut into fingers and bake gently fifteen or twenty minutes.

Gherkin boats are the tiniest kind of bottled gherkins hollowed out and filled with any white savoury mixture and a long strip of red pimento or tomato up the centre.

For *celery boats* choose well-rounded pieces of nice clean celery cut into 1½-inch lengths; *slice a bit off the round side* to make them stand steady and fill them with any savoury mixture. A very distinguished filling for these or any other hollow vegetable is 1 tablespoonful each of stuffed olives, green pepper, onion, cucumber (rind and all) chopped very fine and mingled with cream cheese and mayonnaise. You can top up with a sail of cheese and a couple of sailors of sliced gherkin.

Open sandwiches are small (about 1¼" x ½") oblongs of buttered brown bread spread with anything hot and salty but having no second layer of bread on top. If they are made of little shapes of bread toasted on one side only, spread with the same ingredients on the untoasted side and heated under the grill they are *canapés*. But they are rather more trouble because they won't all go under the grill and some get burned and some aren't very hot, and one way and another they need more watching than a suite of performing fleas. So to keep it nice and simple I keep to my old 'open-faced' sandwiches and just stick new things on them such as:

Sicily sandwich: 8 sardines, 2 hard-boiled yolks, 1½ oz. butter, lemon juice, paprika, nutmeg, pinch of cayenne. Skin, bone and pound sardines with yolks and butter (melted) add lemon and seasonings. Spread liberally on the brown bread rafts and top with a dash of paprika.

Tartare sandwiches: 2 oz. lean cooked ham, 1 gherkin, a few capers, stiff mayonnaise, tarragon vinegar, 1 hard-boiled egg. Chop everything fairly small, bind with mayonnaise and spread thickly on fancy shapes of brown bread and butter.

Devilled sandwiches are chutney, creamed butter, lemon juice, chopped pickled onions and grated cheese, with a dash of curry powder.

Normande sandwiches act fresh shrimps with anchovy paste, cream, and lemon juice.

Portugaise sandwiches are a simple oyster, sat on a well-buttered snippet of brown bread with a squeeze of lemon juice, and either a knob of caviare or a caper beside it, topped with a sprinkle of paprika.

Any of these can be decorated with latticed gherkin or strips of scarlet peppers or white of hard-boiled egg as you please and you may use oddments of salmon or haddock on either the cheese pastry or the brown bread with great effect.

If you want to be very grand and have your snippets hot you merely make the smallest size cases you can from rough puff pastry, heat them before serving and fill them with a mixture of chicken and ham, tongue and hard-boiled egg, salmon, haddock, crab or lobster. Whichever you are using must be well beaten up with rich creamy sauce, *very* well seasoned and heated in a thick saucepan.

Anything goes, in a bouchée, so long as it is hot, creamy and distinctive flavour. If you can also arrange that it is a pretty pink, and where the stuffing gapes forth from under its little hat there is a minute sprig of fresh green parsley or a trio of petits pois, you have scored a culinary bull's-eye. But bouchées should, as their name indicates, be only one mouthful.

Other hot delights are 'Bobs':

Crab: a firm lump of tinned crab wrapped in a tiny jacket of streaky bacon, and grilled.

Cheese: small lump of cheese (half the size of a lump of sugar) wrapped *both* ways, to cover all sides, with bacon and grilled.

Scallop: large cooked scallops cut into same size and treated same way.

Kidney: same thing but brush kidney with butter first. Secure the bacon jacket in each case with a sharpened match or toothpick and leave it in when serving to save burning or greasing the fingers. 'Bobs' should come straight from the grill and the late-comers just go without.

But perhaps the simplest and most classic cocktail sandwich of all goes thus:

Buy a small, very new, brown loaf—even a warm one if you can get it. Remove all crusts with a very sharp saw knife and cut into slices with ditto, spread each with a creamed butter mixed with thick lemony sauce Hollandaise (or mayonnaise if you are lazy). Lay on each slice a small finger of thin tinned asparagus, or, if it is small enough and you have cooked it well, the top part of your garden asparagus. *Roll* the bread round it and before it can unroll pack it in a small tin which is lined with a damp cloth and then with greaseproof paper next to the sandwiches. A small loaf cut thin will make about 15, allowing for you to spoil one or two if it's your first attempt at rolling, and if you leave them until the evening they will be firm and manageable and an acute delight.

Actually you can get by very well on these, with curried dates—cheese straws, and kippers twists if you want to be both distinguished *and* reluctant, and leave the decorations to someone else. But I hope you'll have a shot at them later, because they are incredibly easy and effective and will start any party off with a bang.

For the accompanying fireworks see Chapter 3, headed DRINKS.

3

Drinks

ANY party stands or falls, as much as anything, by the nature and excellence of its drinks. But I'd better begin with some soft ones and warm up gradually. A party isn't necessarily an alcoholic one, and if your taste runs to Bridge Teas and the like we'd better have something about teas first.

It ought to be an insult to you to say that for tea the water must be boiling, the teapot hot and the pot taken to the kettle, *not* the other way round.

All right then, go on and be insulted, but I know hundreds of people who pay no attention to the last bit. And if they warm the teapot they warm it *wet* instead of putting it on the hot rack above the kettle to warm *dry*.

You already know about not using an aluminium kettle, which if your water is softened (as I hope for your sake it

20

is) will make a horrible greyish brew of peculiar flavour. I am no chemist and have never worked this one out, but I know that softened water has a most destructive effect on galvanized pipes and assume that in the kettle it does a bit of aluminium-eating to the subsequent destruction of your tea by the addition of the stuff it stewed out of the metal.

So iron or tin kettles please, and soft water; and half the usual quantity of tea.

I never heard such nonsense as 'one for each person and one for the pot'. Three spoonfuls for four people gives you 8 large breakfast cups. Pour a little water on first, wait for a moment while the leaves swell and the kettle re-boils, and then fill up the pot. And before pouring out remember to *warm each cup* with hot water then pour into the slop bowl. If I could persuade you to try tea made this way and with no sugar or milk you would know what tea really tasted like. It is a glorious beverage, as stimulating as hock and not unlike it if you use green tea or a good hill-grown Darjeeling variety. Tea has such a delicate flavour that to make a kind of inferior soup by adding sugar and milk seems to me to conceal it completely. If you *must* add anything, float a lump of lemon on top and use one lump of sugar. That is quite delicious and you can still taste the tea.

However, there are those who prefer a brand yielding the greatest quantity of the blackest tea from the least number of spoonfuls. If you are not sure *how* debased the palate of your guests may be, or if you want to keep all your beautiful green tea to yourself, make a brew of Ceylon as well and offer them a choice. If they decide on Ceylon and put milk in it, it doesn't matter so much, it is fairly foolproof.

But I will allow you even sugary milky tea if you will be sensible about the coffee.

Buy it hot from the roaster and store it in an *airtight* jar. Grind enough each time (one tablespoonful of beans per half-pint of coffee) and no more, and for the breakfast coffee do the grinding at night and cover the result with enough *top-off the milk* to soak it.

No I have *not* mixed up two recipes.

And you soak the evening coffee all day.

This utterly priceless piece of information was given to me by an eminent professor of chemistry who explained that the fat in the milk draws out the best part of the coffee, which otherwise goes down the drain.

And my goodness he's right.

Here I am living right next door to Grasse, smothered in perfume factories and had neglected to apply one of their elementary principles to the most cherished operation in my kitchen.

In perfume-making the more delicate flowers, jasmine and tuberose and orange blossom, are what Bacon called 'fast of their smel' and decline to yield up any perfume if boiled like the commoner blooms. But each day's intake of these precious ones is laid on trays of fat (mixed beef and pork fat) in a thin layer and by next morning the fat has subtly extracted the scent which no harsh treatment could unloose.

In the same way the coffee perfume—the most delightful part—is left largely unmoved by the attack of boiling water, and firmly locked within the gritty fragments it is thrown away. Whereas if soaked all night in fatty milk it is subtly extracted into the liquid and you can then proceed according

to which is your favourite method, filter or saucepan.

I do it thus and people (any people, all people) say quite unsolicited, that they never tasted the like. You'd better check up on it just to see that they're speaking the truth, it's a thing that's worth getting right, reputations as a hostess have been made—or ruined—just by coffee before today.

Very well then, grind your coffee and put it last night into an enamelled saucepan with the top off a quart of milk. This morning add half a pint of water to every tablespoonful of coffee in the pan and a pinch of salt. (If you live on the Mediterranean make it a *very* small pinch because I never *knew* such strong salt. But if you live there you can make coffee anyhow, without any presumptuous aid from me.) Bring this slowly to the boil (whatever it was I was talking about) and when it has bubbled to the top of the pan remove it and let it bubble down again. Do this three times, swirl it round with a spoon, let a few drops from the cold tap run on to it to carry down the sediment (because cold water is heavier than hot I understand and in descending takes the grounds with it), and after standing it on the plate-rack where the coffee-jug is waiting, while you heat a little milk, pour all but the dregs into the jug and take it and the milk in to breakfast quickly.

If you must have your coffee black it is very tiresome but here you are:

Have a coffee-pot with a filter top with freshly ground coffee and a pinch of salt. Pour on about half a coffee-cupful of boiling water and leave it in a warm place a moment to swell. Now fill up the filter top and leave it ten minutes to drip through.

Discard filter and take to table.

There are also other harmless mildly alcoholic beverages very easily prepared and useful for buffet drinks in summertime, or for juvenile dances, as for instance:

Hock Cup

1 bottle hock (Empire will do)
½ gill of curacao
½ gill of dry sherry
1 gill of brandy
1 pint soda water
1 cupful ice cubes
borage leaves to float on top

Claret Cup: This is the same recipe with the addition of ½ gill lemon juice and a few slices of cucumber.

Cider Cup

a quart flagon of medium sweet cider
2 gills bitter beer
1 gill pale sherry
½ gill brandy
½ gill orange curacao
½ gill rum
rind in strips and squeezed juice of one lemon and one orange.
1 cupful of ice in cubes

Here follow half a dozen surprisingly good and quite non-alcoholic cups guaranteed simultaneously to quench the thirst, make glad the heart and leave the head unimpaired.

Strawberry Cup: 2 lb. strawberries crushed, covered with water and ½ lb. sugar and left until next day. Strain into a bowl, add 1 tin pineapple juice, 1 dozen each whole strawberries, pineapple cubes and ice cubes and 1 quart good cider.

Orange Cup

1 cupful ice cubes
1 pint orange juice
1 gill lemon juice
1 gill syrup from sugar
   cubes

1 bottle apple juice
1 siphon soda water.
   Decorate with borage
   flowers.

Teapunch: 1 quart water and 1 lb. sugar boiled with the rind of 2 lemons for five minutes. 2 cups of strong tea (3 teaspoonfuls of tea), juice of three lemons, juice of two large grapefruit, chill and serve with equal parts of chilled ginger ale.

Ginger Cordial: Very good hot for winter and iced for summer.

4 drachms essence of
capsicum
4 drachms essence of ginger
2 drachms essence of lemon

2 drachms essence of
burnt sugar
1 oz. tartaric acid

On 2 lb. of loaf sugar pour a quart of boiling water and add the above mixture, but do not add tartaric until cold. Bottle and use 2 tablespoonfuls to a tumbler, filling up with hot or cold water.

Lemonade

1 bottle lemon essence	1 oz. citric acid
1 lb. loaf sugar	

Mix in a large jug with boiling water. Bottle when cold, and when required put 1 inch in bottom of tumbler and dilute with iced water to taste.

Spiced Fruitade for 6

1 cup orange juice	Juice of 1 lemon and
1 cup pineapple juice	peeled rind
1 cup syrup (2 parts	½ teaspoon nutmeg
water and 1 part sugar	½ teaspoon cinnamon
boiled together	3 whole cloves

Chill for three hours, then strain into wide-mouthed jug containing ice and one large bottle sweet cider. Let lemon peel float on top with blue borage flowers.

Mulled Wine for Twelfth Night for six is a good hot drink. Make a brew of *China* tea. Put a bottle of the cheapest red table wine you can find, Algerian claret or any of those curious things you find at the grocer's (only *not* British Port Type) in a large saucepan, add 2 breakfastcups of the China tea, ½ pint bitter beer, 1 sherry glass of rum, 6 whole cloves, a ½ teaspoonful each of cinnamon and nutmeg and the thinly peeled rind of an orange. Put it at the back of a stove for as long as you like. It must never actually *boil*, only *poach*. And when you serve it don't forget to put a silver spoon in each glass to absorb the heat.

If you feel this is beneath your notice as a punch try this one, the classic recipe:

½ pint brandy
½ pint rum
2 small lemons
½ boiling water

3 oz. loaf sugar
a pinch each cinnamon
  and nutmeg

Rub the rough sugar lumps on the lemon until all rind is scratched off. Melt sugar in the liquid over fire. Put this and all the other ingredients into a hot punch-bowl, add the strained lemon juice and serve at once.

Whisky Punch

2 pints old ale
1 gill rum
1 gill gin
¼ lb. sugar.
1 pint boiling water

1 gill Irish whisky
1 sliced lemon
a pinch of powdered
  cinnamon, nutmeg and
  cloves.

Melt all the liquids, sugar and spices in a large saucepan until almost boiling. Pour into punch-bowl, add sliced lemon and ladle into glasses.

Peppermint cup is a cold punch. Chill a tall white glass; half-fill it with chipped ice. Add a tablespoonful of crème de menthe and ½ a gill of gin. Fill up with ginger beer and put a sprig of frosted mint on top.

Party punch

1 quart cider
2 gills sherry

1 gill brandy
1 gill gin

Slices of lime, lemon and orange, fresh mint and fruit cubes (made from orange juice and sugar put in the ice-tray and frozen as usual). Stand in frig. for an hour. Put 2 small or 1 large cube in each glass, half-fill with punch and add iced soda water to taste.

Pimm's Punch: For each person ⅔ gill Pimm's No. 1, ⅓ gin, 3 dashes angostura, squeeze of lemon and one slice of lemon, 2 slices of cucumber, 2 lumps of ice, and a gill of champagne. Ladle into goblets, top with soda water, toss a bit of mint in, then sniff and drink. It's rather like drinking from a water-lily pond with a fountain, and just as cooling.

We have now painlessly graduated out of the harmless beverage class and will begin on a course of Short Drinks presenting a few easy cocktails. All my own work and labelled according to virtue. G.C. = good and cheap. G. and *V.*C. = good and *very* cheap. G.F. = good and fierce, and N.N. = not for novices.

1. ½ gin   1 teaspoonful sugar-syrup
    ½ raspberry juice   G.C.

                    ★   ★   ★

2. ½ gin   1 teaspoon syrup
    ½ tangerine juice   1 curacao   G.C.

                    ★   ★   ★

3. ⅓ French vermouth   ⅓ bitter beer
    ⅓ Irish whisky   G.F.

                    ★   ★   ★

4. ⅓ rum   dash of orange bitters and
    ⅓ grapefruit juice   spoonful sugar
    ⅓ sherry   G.F.

                    ★   ★   ★

5. 1 part British sherry   1 part orange squash.
    1 part gin   G.C

                    ★   ★   ★

6. 1 part British sherry   1 part *bitter* beer
    1 part orange squash   G. and V.C.

                    ★   ★   ★

7. 1 part gin   twist of orange peel
    1 part orange squash   and ice well in a large glass
    2 parts cider with a   G. and V.C.

                    ★   ★   ★

8. 1 part gin   2 parts bitter beer, ice well
    1 part orange squash   with a twist of peel G.C.

All the foregoing will do very well after a tennis-party
or church bazaar or any place where they are liable to be
very thirsty for a long time.

The following are not so well adapted for drinking in
great quantity.

9. 1 part gin   ½ part Graves
    1 part cointreau   1 part gin
    1 part lemon squash   1 part orange juice
    ½ part absinthe   G.F.

★　　★　　★

10. 1part French Vermouth   ½ part curacao, twist of peel
　　 ½ part Italian   N.N.

★　　★　　★

11. 1 part gin   1 part orange squash
　　 1 part French Vermouth   dash of orange bitters
　　 1 part bitter beer   N.N.

★　　★　　★

12. 1 part East India sherry   1 part bitter beer and dash
　　 1 part gin   of orange bitters
　　 1 part cointreau   N.N.

★　　★　　★

13. 1 part gin   1 part bitter beer and twist
　　 1 part orange squash   orange peel
　　 1 part curacao   G.F. and N.N.

★　　★　　★

14. 1 part rum   1 part bitter beer and peel
　　 1 part orange squash   N.N.

★　　★　　★

15. 1 part brandy   1 part British sherry
　　 1 part cider   G.F.

★　　★　　★

16. 1 part French vermouth   1 part strong black coffee
     1 part gin   Dash of orange bitters and
     1 part brandy   a twist of tangerine peel
                                                 G.F.

★   ★   ★

17. 1 part gin   1 part lemon squash and
  1 part cointreau   twist of peel   N.N.

★   ★   ★

18. 1 part Tio Pepe   Twist of orange peel
     1 part gin   G.F. and N.N
     1 part curacao

★   ★   ★

19. 1 part Irish whisky   1 part bitter beer
     1 part Kummel   G.F. and N.N.

There are any number of more orthodox cocktails but they are no better than these and usually more expensive. I specify British sherry because its alcoholic content is greater in ratio to its price than any other beverage except home-distilled brandy. And I recommend bitter beer because—well, try it and see. But you will notice that the range of ingredients is deliberately kept very limited because most cocktail books assume that you have unlimited hoards of strange liqueurs, spirits, bitters, beverages and nostrums of every kind, tucked away just waiting to be tossed about. A very fallacious theory so far as most households are concerned, and the more you can do in the way of cocktails with very limited ingredients the less complicated life will be.

For more serious and formal entertaining there are a few facts which should be graven on every hostess's heart and the sooner we learn them the more carefree will be the ensuing entertainment.

For weddings and celebrations serve champagne.

With beef, mutton, lamb, duck, hare or venison use a red wine—claret or Burgundy. It will have a sediment which is stirred by travelling, therefore let it rest twenty-four hours on its side before serving. Draw the cork gently without shaking the bottle and leave it uncorked, in the room where it is to be drunk. Serve in a large globular glass only half-full, to give the bouquet room to rise. With fish, poultry, veal, or pork, serve a white wine—a hock, Graves, White Burgundy, Moselle—draw the cork and put in a refrigerator for about half an hour. Serve in a long-stemmed glass.

Sherry before a meal should be pale and dry and after it dark and sweet. Did you know that the dark rich 'East India' sherries are so styled, not because the vines grew in India or the wine ever set foot on Indian shores but because the big casks full of it were sent on a voyage round the Cape in the East India merchant ships, to age and mellow it before it was considered fit to drink.

Port comes after dessert, with the cheese, and liqueurs come with the coffee.

Now for a home-made drink to end all drinks, from the cellar-book of my grandfather. I could show you the very cellar. And I am sure they made and *drank* it because of the thumbed appearance of the page. But regarded coldly it might seem more fitted to elevate aeroplanes than the human heart. It comes in the category F.H. (Fit for Heroes).

To twenty gallons of clean rectified spirits put six ounces of sweet spirits of nitre, six ounces of pounded bitter almonds, half an ounce of sliced orris root and six prune stones pounded. Agitate the whole well together two or three times a day for three days.

Let it settle and then pour in one quart of the best wine vinegar and add to every four gallons one gallon of foreign brandy.

After that it seems to me the last word on drinks has been magnificently said. There isn't a thing one can add, except—what on earth were six prune stones doing in that company?

To sum up: for all cocktails economy is fatal. Spare the gin and spoil the party.

With cocktails and canapés your hot should be hot and your cold cold but never the twain should meet, so see that the bouchées are kept in the oven until the last moment and the iced drinks taken out of the frigidaire only when the first guest arrives at the door.

A nice topping for a cocktail is frosted mint: cook ¼ lb. loaf sugar and two tablespoonfuls of water until it candies and then when slightly cool dip the young mint leaves in and lay on a tray to stiffen.

For the first cocktail dip top edge of glass in a saucer of green sugar made by mixing a few drops of green dye with granulated sugar and drying it out again.

No half-measures with the flavourings. They must be distinctive. So must the cocktails.

But don't overdo it. Because a given quantity of curry or anchovy is to your taste, double quantity is not necessarily twice as good. And that goes for orange bitters too.

And while we're talking about drink *do* remember to draw the cork of the Burgundy in the morning and leave it on the sideboard, otherwise you'll have to warm it in a hurry and end up with mulled wine.

Did you ever have trouble remembering whose glass was whose? Then paint on the bottom of each one before arrival the Christian name of the guest in nail lacquer. That's about the only kind of paint that will withstand a cocktail.

Or, if you are using tumblers, crochet a different-coloured 'coaster' for each one in rows of coloured wool. Everyone can memorize their own colours (so long as they are in a condition to do any memorizing) and after that they will neither know nor care.

Crochet is a way of enclosing a lot of air with a little wool so that it makes something to put round something else. People do it to each other at Christmas-time in the form of tea cosies, slippers, hot-water bottle thingummies and shoulder shawls for reading in bed. But as coasters it is both useful and ornamental, allowing one to get a better hold on the glass and eliminating the danger of scratches on grand pianos, where glasses frequently come to roost.

To make one coaster. Take several colours of wool and use, one at a time, with a crochet hook. Make a ring of five chain. (This is not a square-dancing instruction.) Into this hole, do one-treble-three chain five times and join. Do six chain and then put a treble into the centre chain of your first effort in the last row, three chain and a treble into the first *treble* of last row, three chain and a treble all round until you have ten trebles (I *think*. Anyhow you have plenty) with chain between. Do this multiplication some more if you must but I should think the circle would now be the diameter of the glass bottom. If so, continue doing rows with the same number of stitches and a different-coloured wool for three rows. Swap wools again and add an extra treble and three chain at beginning of row, and again half-way round, to allow for expansion of the glass. The idea is to get about half-way up the glass and make a nicely tailored striped jacket for it, but you can go up as far as you like or stop right now, so far as I am concerned.

If you are a real crocheter you can do nimble variations that look like demented butterflies. My kind looks like wire netting because I never got beyond the first lesson but I can tell you that so far as jackets for glasses are concerned they are a very valuable thing to know.

Particularly if the drink is hot.

4

The Festive Board

I DON'T know why any difficulty ever arose as to the proper position for table cutlery. You work out what is likely to be eaten and put the necessary implements in the most convenient positions and the order in which you will need them.

Thus, at a formal dinner-party calling for soup, fish, meat sweet and cheese, the soup spoon would be the outside tool on the right hand because you need it first, then comes the fish knife with the corresponding fork on the outside left. Inside these again come the large knife (right) and fork (left) for meat and the small cheese knife on the inside right again, to butter your roll (if any), whose plate rests at the extreme left and bears a folded napkin. In the old ornate days napkins were tortured to look like water lilies, mitres, fans, shells, rabbits, roses, boars' heads or slippers, and lurking somewhere inside them would be a roll. Nowadays life is not long enough, and plate, napkin, roll, lie chaste and severe one upon the other in stark and Gothic nudity. Across the top lie your spoon (handle pointing to the right because you will use it in that hand) and fork (handle to the left).

If you want to know why these two don't form the innermost rank at the side, it is because enough is enough and any more implements there would take up too much room. Better have them out of the way at the top.

You might be serving a chilled grapefruit before the soup.
Never mind, the grapefruit in its glass arrives on a plate,
with the teaspoon for eating it ready beside it.

And if you are being really formal and delivering finger-
bowls on the dessert plates, lift off the bowl and place it
top-left of your plate, to balance the wine glasses on the
right.

With these too it is entirely a question of convenience.
The one you need first, probably sherry with the soup, is
nearest your hand, the hock or whatnot for the main course
next to it, and a small one, either liqueur, port or one for
brown sherry according to what is coming, furthest away.

Table laying, like etiquette and the Highway Code, is
just a matter of common sense and a fellow-feeling for
your fellow-man. If you make things as convenient as you
can for everyone you're pretty sure to be right. Though if
you had lived in the late 1800's eating out might have been
a shade more complicated.

My mother's copy of *Warne's Everyday Cookery* says:
Dinner-parties of the present day are rendered much
less expensive affairs than they used to be, by the
fashion of serving them in the Russian style. The
regular dinner *à la russe* is served thus:

Either a silver or glass plateau runs down the centre
of the table, or a handsome centre-piece of plate is
placed in the middle of it, such as a silver tree, with
figures or animals at the foot of it; or a raised centre
dessert dish, containing fruit, flowers, etc., etc. Round
this centre are small glass dishes of preserves; outside,
alternate dishes of fruit, and vases of flowers with

occasional bottles of sherry, and carafes of water with their several tumblers on them, a finger glass holding a wine glass to each plate. In short, the table is made to look as handsome as possible with glass, plate, etc., etc. In each plate is a 'carte' of the dinner.

The dishes are brought in and placed on the sideboard or on a side table. The soup is handed round, then the fish; then the side dishes or entrées. Next the removes, as turkey, roast saddle of mutton, etc., etc., ready carved, of course, and on the plate. Then comes the second course, i.e. game, or duck, or artichokes, puddings, jelly, cream, tarts, etc.; next, cheese, macaroni, celery, etc.

The butler goes round with the wine as usual—sherry, champagne, hock, etc., etc,—between the courses.

Then the servants place the dessert plates, etc., and retire.

A much less number of dishes is required for this style of dinner, than were needed when it was usual to place them on the table. Dinner is more rapidly served; and each dish is handed hot, and at the moment it should be eaten.'

We will try to forget about the glories of the past and adhere firmly to the present.

In laying a table for dinner you have two choices—modern style, in which you use peasant pottery, brightly checked tablecloth, coloured glass, an amusing centrepiece and great informality—and classic, which calls for a large, stiff, snowy cloth, winking silver, cut glass, pure beeswax candles in crystal or silver holders, and a great deal of decorum.

But even in the latter case you can save yourself a great deal of work by bringing in everything on a trolley, finishing off one place at a time, measuring off another, 24 inches from it (if you don't want your guests to be nudging each other all the time) and repeat the process until you have no more utensils, space or guests.

Allow a small pepper and salt to each two people, spoons for serving alongside the mats which will later bear hot dishes, a few dishes of olives and salted almonds and a centrepiece which is beautiful but refined.

Carving is easiest to do on a side table and the hostess will be served last. In the hazardous years of Chapter 1

page 1, the host or hostess was always served first, but that was only an insurance policy on the lives of dubious but well-informed guests.

Such precautions are now unnecessary.

One still endeavours to arrange the seating male, female, male, female, all round the table and to ensure for everyone's sake that husbands and wives do *not* sit together. The most important lady sits at the host's right hand and the next in importance on his left, reversing the sexes at the other end with the most exalted gentleman on the hostess's right. And she must give them an indication as to their seats on entering the dining-room, saying firmly 'Will you sit here, Sir Henry, Doctor, here; you, Uncle, over there; and Bobby in the middle'; rather than letting them shuffle about without a clue. After all *someone* has to guide them and she must be firm.

However, extreme formality and exactitude of placing is now largely abandoned, except at diplomatic functions and if you are ever in doubt as to the precise eminence of a batch of Excellencies consult the Foreign Office and have your seating plan vetted.

One lingering custom remains.

The hostess tries to avoid finishing before her guests and must toy with a square inch of haddock or remnant of old rook until the assembled jaws are still. Only then may she proceed with the next course.

You have some suggested menus in the preceding chapter.

For ease and convenience, whether you have, or lack, resident maids, I would suggest simplicity and restraint rather than the attack of exhibitionism which all too frequently seizes the hostess and is so unnecessary.

I knew a charming lady who could only cook one thing—steak and kidney pudding, but did that prevent her from having dinner-parties? By no means. She glorified and improved upon that pudding and made of its concoction and distribution such a ritual that one left feeling that it had been a banquet.

And such was the excellence of the cooking and the perfection of the table that it *was*.

Lunches are just the same as dinners though not quite so *much* so, and teas we have already considered under the heading of 'food'. It only remains to give a few hints for buffet meals.

Here convenience is everything. One should be able to grab a plate, move up and down the table selecting this and that, and then make a quick getaway without holding up the traffic. So the food and implements should be well spread out to keep the crowd on the move.

Way back out of the danger line of mayonnaise and bowls of cream you need flowers, and as they will be against a wall and probably in a corner they may be high and fussy if you feel that way.

Or they may just be amusing, like a Japanese garden in a square pottery pudding dish with real water and tiny rose trees. But don't try too hard to be realistic with this one, as I did, by putting baby frogs in the little lily-pool whose 'lilies' were apple blossom. Frogs can jump and it wasn't so much those we retrieved out of the salad, the butter, and the trifle, which worried me—it was the one we never found at all.

Everything on a buffet should be gay and jolly and colourful because it's that kind of party and, anyway, one eats with the eyes as much as the palate. Use a generous assortment of coloured vegetables and fruits, and frivolous sweets and savouries in green, red, orange, black and pink. The invaluable 'Warne' says:

> A lady has full space for exercising her taste at the supper table. A good eye for colour will give a great charm to the arrangement. With flowers, fruit, frothed whipped creams, coloured jellies, and all the elegance of sweet dishes she can scarcely fail to offer a perfect picture of gastronomic beauty to the eye.
>
> A plan drawn out on paper and given to an intelligent servant will secure her from mistakes generally, but if her footman is inexperienced she should just glance at the table herself before the guests are invited in.

You already in Chapter 2 met some salads and savouries for buffet suppers, with risotto, goulash, curry or spaghetti dishes, which will keep hot on top of the stove until the last moment. There should also be one or two good iced layer cakes, lemon meringue pie, trifles, jellies and fruit salads, with bowls of potato crisps, asparagus and canned sweet corn, as well as small hot rolls. These are very easy to make at home and wrapped in a towel out of draughts will keep warm for hours. Use:

1½ oz. yeast	2 cups of lukewarm milk
1 teaspoon salt	¼ cup sugar

Blend these, add 2 beaten eggs and 3 cups flour sifted in. Add half-cup of melted marg. beat well until smooth and add rest of flour. Let it rise in a warm place and punch it down. Rise again, knead again and make walnut-sized rolls. Let it rise again and bake fifteen minutes at 375°F. Leave them in the pans covered with a cloth in a warm place until wanted. This quantity is enough for twenty guests and they are much, *much* lighter and more appetizing than the commercial variety.

At one end of the buffet spread out your silver in a beautiful shining fan-shaped array—all the forks together, all the spoons, large spoons for serving and a group of sauces and condiments. There should be a spoon and fork for each person, a cutting knife with each cake, a serving spoon and fork beside each dish, a butter knife on the butter dish, a pile of plates with a small napkin on each plate, and the tea and coffee (with spoons in saucers) at one end to balance the hard drinks at the other.

All they have to do now is grab a plate and a fork, select from each dish what pleases them and mingle it on the plate—butter a roll and balance this, a cup or a glass, and the heaped plate, as they steer a tricky course back to their seat through a milling crowd of other hungry ones. But it might be much worse. You can even eat a buffet supper sitting on the floor, and frequently *have* to. You can't do that with 'joint and two veg'.

For cocktail-parties the buffet is similar but slighter. An amusing array of bits and pieces is flanked by works of art like cabbage porcupines.

Stick a couple of good-sized hard-hearted cabbages all over in diagonal lines with snacks on cocktail sticks thus: pull down the outer leaves, remove a few of the next layers, and on the smooth, pale green heart impale candy-striped rows of prawns, bits of cheese, stuffed dates, twirls of anchovy, angels on horseback, stuffed olives and so on. Each row should be a distinct colour and a different taste.

Have also a couple of large—very large—old-fashioned meat dishes with a tureen or other receptacle-on-a-stand in the centre. Round the edge pile heaps of dill pickles, chips, prawns, cheese sticks, pieces of crab, olives and rolled anchovies in sections, and in the tureen put tomato sauce or mayonnaise, shrimp sauce or garlic sauce, so that the hungry may take up each morsel on one of the sticks provided, twirling it in the sauce and popping it into the waiting mouth.

You already know some good savoury snacks and canapés to make, and here are some good sandwich fillings:

> Cheese and bacon
> Smoked salmon and egg
> Apple and peanut butter
> Cheese and marmalade
> Liver and bacon
> Raw kipper fillet and mayonnaise
> Egg and bacon
> Roast beef and horse-radish sauce
> Crab meat and mayonnaise
> Boiled beef with mustard

> Sausage and apple sauce
> Liver sausage and chopped olives
> Prune and nut

Provide as many of these as you can on 'open-faced' sandwiches as well as all the usual pastes and meats and delicacies, inside thinly cut and well-buttered bread, remembering that a sandwich must be moist.

But if you have the ordinary kind of enclosed sandwiches, *label* them or make it otherwise obvious as to exactly what lurks within them, or you will find the guests behaving like a blue-tit on a bird-table—an average of three peeks to a peck.

You can still have your iced layer cakes for those who like sweet things—tinned asparagus, cheese straws, kipper twists or anything you fancy from Chapter 2 and if people don't seem to be helping themselves at a sufficient rate, circulate dishes of mixed tit-bits every quarter of an hour or so and keep the coasters coasting.

And if you think this is rather a bother and you'd prefer something simpler be thankful that you are not obliged to cater according to Wame—whose table for a winter supper was laid out thus:

Winter Supper.

Soup (White Soup).

Turkey.

Ham.

Raised Périgord Pie.

Christmas Cake.

Trifle.

Larded Pheasants.

Tipsy Cake. Gâteau Nourmahal.

Grouse.

Mayonnaise de Poulet.

Oranges.   Oranges.

Custards.

Centre Ornament.

Custards.

Oranges.   Oranges.

Italian Salad.

Capon.

Partridges.

Trifle.

Twelfth Cake.

Vols-au-Vent of Chicken.

Ham.

Christmas Pie.

Partridges.

Pheasants.

Jardinière Soupe.

Left side dishes:

Tarlets à la Crème. Noyau Jelly. Pigeon Pie.

Preserved Ginger.

Almond Gaufres. Dominoes. Blancmange.

Salmi of Game. Open Jelly with Whipped Cream. Roasted Oysters.

Alexander Jelly. Neapolitan Pastry. Chickens.

Ribbon Blanc-mange. Oranges with Jelly. Scalloped Oysters.

Maids of Honour. Orange Chips. Orange Jelly. Mutton Cutlets à la Soubise.

Right side dishes:

Orange Chips. Ice Plum Pudding.

Lemon Jelly. Pigeon Pie.

Flummery. Ribbon Jelly. Scalloped Oysters.

Brunswick Jelly. Chocolate Cakes. Chickens.

Salmi of Game. Open Jelly with Whipped Cream. Roasted Oysters.

Candied Fruit. Vanilla Cream. Almond Gaufres. Dominoes. Blancmange. Punch Jelly. Mutton Cutlets à la Soubise.

5

The Three Rs: Running Repairs and Routine

IT is well known that though a house may conduct itself normally with the smoothness of warm honey and the equilibrium of a gyroscope you have only to contemplate a party for the whole thing either to fall down or blow up.

It is against the malignity of inanimate objects that we now propose to conduct a cunning campaign—either to forestall the arrival of disaster or to conceal its presence—so that the harassed hostess can keep her mind on the human element, which, goodness knows, is enough, without the walls and furniture joining in league against her.

This is, in fact, First Aid for the Home, and to make for

order and brevity we will attack it alphabetically, so that the first item is:

Air. Too many houses are, as a celebrated architect said of an equally celebrated museum, 'a receptacle for the retention and preservation of antiquated air'. The essence of a good party is to keep things moving and that goes for the atmosphere too. More at this time than any other, because an abundance of bodies use oxygen and distribute CO_2 at a more than normal rate. If you have a fireplace, with or without a fire, and an open window, you are being quite scientific without knowing it, and even if you *can* feel the passage of air currents they won't necessarily give you a stiff neck. On the other hand, if you stop every crack and produce a level, static temperature in unstirred air you are quite certain to produce a cold. Moreover, it is the ideal medium in which to incubate a ravaging crop of germs, so that whatever of one sort or another of bacteria any guests import, will be hatched and distributed to an alarming degree before they leave.

Play for safety and leave a window open. And if you are uncertain about the general temperature of your rooms at normal times use pot plants as miners use white mice. See what happens to them and if they flourish it's all right for *you*. But if they die you'd better do something about it.

AIRLOCK IN THE HOT-WATER SYSTEM. This is a most disturbing derangement of the domestic machine and commonly happens after a freeze-up or other blockage of the pipes so that water has been drawn off without being replaced by anything but air.

Use a short piece of garden hose. Ram one end on the

main cold tap and the other on the hot. Open both taps and
hold the hose on to them tightly. If it doesn't blow off, the
cold water will force its way up the hot pipe and blow out
the bubbles. If it *does*, you change and begin all over again.
If a minion or serf can listen near the hot tank they will
hear the bubbles blowing. After a few minutes of this,
release the pent-up water and let it flow out, otherwise the
tank will become too full and you are landed with too much
water rather than none at all. If airlock persists, do it again,
but once is usually enough. I have known tyros at this
ingenious bit of plumbing practice who said that it was
more than enough. But that was their fault, not mine.

ARRANGEMENTS FOR A PARTY. Don't leave everything
for the day itself. In fact, don't leave *anything* to do on
that day which can be equally well done in advance. See
that the silver is cleaned and all the necessary bits and
pieces back from the laundry. Look round, pretending to
be a guest, and see if there is anything to criticize. The
normal self-hypnotism of any housewife has persuaded you,
up to now, that all was well. But if you discard the rose-
coloured periscope of affection and acquaintance and look
through the quizzing-glass of a rival hostess you will see
that walls are leprous, cushions moulting, chintz long past
its first youth, paint dim and carpet downtrodden. Do
something about it while there is yet time.

Cook your cold soup on Thursday and the rest of your
cooking on Friday and keep in the refrigerator or wrapped
in tinfoil, for a party on Saturday. Have your hair set the
day before and if you are proposing to wear new shoes
there is only one word for it. Don't. But if you must, wear

them for an hour or two on the previous evenings.

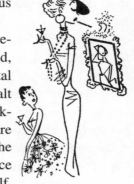

Make out a list several days before-hand of the things you will need, otherwise you may find at the fatal moment that you have no coffee or salt or bread—no tin-opener or no cork-screw. And do sit down while you are cutting sandwiches or by the time the party starts the only comfortable place for your feet will be on the mantelshelf.

Arrange the furniture to make the most room and the fewest obstacles. And *dont forget* to dust the tops of pictures and high shelves, even if you can't see them. Some of the guests may be taller than you.

BEDROOM, comfort of. If guests are remaining overnight, do see that the bed is well aired and comfortable. Everyone has experienced at some time or another the chill and rocky horror of a 'spare bed'. In the name of hospitality do what you can to mitigate this. The French kind of bed, made of sheep's wool over a core of horse hair and re-made every three years is the ideal; if you can't get this have a 'pocketed spring' type which comes up smiling after years of wear and any weight. See that there are flowers, ample towels, clothes-brush, writing-paper, ash-tray, box of biscuits, ample clothes-hangers, waste-paper basket, easy chair, light reading, reading-light and an eiderdown. And see that the light is suitable both for the dressing-table and reading in bed. If not, move either or both of them. You can't move the light, and there is nothing more

THE THREE RS: RUNNING REPAIRS AND ROUTINE

exasperating to a guest than being unable to see (*a*) her nose, and (*b*) her book, however unworthy of regard either of them may actually be.

BLACK SUIT, TO RESTORE. Put it on and get someone to run over you with the vacuum cleaner.

BLACK LACE, TO REFRESH. Make a big bold brew of tea, enough to cover the article and steep for twelve hours, dipping and dabbling and generally fussing at it every time you happen to think of it. Pound an ounce of gum arabic and dissolve it in a pint of water. Squeeze the lace out of the tea and douse it in the gum, then put it in a towel and bang it gently about for ten minutes or so. If it is still worth doing anything about, spread it on a towel (another one I mean, *dry*) and pin it straight or curly or however you want it to go. Put it on a thorn bush to dry if you have one; if not, use a clothes airer and when nearly dry put another towel on top of it, the third in this series, and iron it with a fairly cool iron. There are people who swear by a beer-bath instead of tea, in which case no gum is needed.

BLANKETS TO WASH. When washed and dried, make a spirited attack on the blanket (while still hanging on the line) with a carpet-beater. This brings up the pristine fluffy surface and prevents that jaded, felted, down-in-the-mouth look that home-laundered blankets normally wear.

BURST PIPES. If this has happened to you I can think of no more hampering catastrophe. Turn off the stopcock on the main supply, keep only a very small fire and call the plumber. If you can't find the stopcock, tie up the ball-valve in the tank (you will find it roosting in the most inaccessible

portion of the roof); this will stop any more water from flowing in and curb the flood.

CARPET, TO CLEAN. Routine refreshment. Wring out a cloth in ammonia, tie it over a broom or mop head and rub it all over the carpet once a month. A sprinkle of common salt brushed all over the carpet helps to bring up the colours and keep away moths. If there is a worn patch where you can neither stand something on it nor slew round the carpet to put it in a far corner, an emergency repair which works quite well is to paint on the pattern again with ordinary builders' oil paint and allow it twenty-four hours to dry. If you mix shreds of cotton-wool with the paint it will take off the nap-less look.

CHIMNEY SMOKING. The wind bloweth where it listeth and more often than not it will blow for 364 days of the year and be listless on the day of your party. Give the wretched thing all the draught you can from below, light a newspaper up the chimney to get the air currents moving in the right direction, and lay some lighting-wood or other inflammable material on top of the coal to pull the heat through and make a bright clear fire. Next day get the builder to fit a 'cowl' or add two or three courses of brickwork to the chimney head, to increase the pulling power of the draught. If chimney top is below the level of roof ridge no wonder the poor thing smokes. Every wandering breeze cascades straight off the roof and down it. If the fireplace is back-to-back with another, stuff the *other* one with a sack or something. If still obdurate it may be a starling's nest in which case stuff the starling. Pending the arrival of builders' ladders, have the party in the kitchen and pretend that it was your idea all along, as being more original and less formal.

CEILINGS, TO PAPER. The preliminary decorations may include the refreshment of a ceiling, in which case I pity you. It is best (if there can be said to be any best about this business at all) to use a ceiling distemper, of which there are many proprietary brands. If ceiling is cracked or otherwise un-ceilworthy you'll have to use paper. Recipe for paste will be found later under PASTE. Slap it evenly and not too thick on to plain white paper and fold the paper into a 'concertina', sticky to sticky, in folds of not more than 18 inches. This is easier to carry up the steps than a long strip. Get the end straight with the angle of ceiling and wall and un-concertina it a bit at a time as you press it to the ceiling surface with a dry, clean distemper brush. Have someone down below to hold the steps. Better still, *you* hold the steps and let the other one go up with the paper.

CHAIR LEGS, TO MEND. It is sometimes necessary to review the probable hazards attendant on bulky guests who always choose the most unworthy chairs on which to repose. I am all for a laugh and a joke but to be really jolly it must be shared by all, therefore I say, have a look at all the chair legs in your preliminary survey and if any are cracked mend them thus: bind the affected part with a splint of string or carpet thread and cover it well with glue. If a plain sort of chair with straight insides to its leg, screw a metal angle strip along it, half on the leg, half on the seat; it will then hold an elephant if such a thing should be necessary. If the leg, owing to some previous impact, is *already* broken, glue both the broken edges and leave to become tacky, then cut off the head of a wire nail with the pliers and sharpen it to a point with a file. Drive one end into one of the broken surfaces and bang the other broken bit on to the end you have just pointed. It will thus be both glued and 'bradded' and you can proceed to glue the outside and do the splinting mentioned above. It is on the same principle as one puts a metal pin in a broken leg. If you can leave the leg (the chair leg of course) clamped in a vice all night so much the firmer.

CHIMNEY ON FIRE. This may be the result of your capers with newspaper up the chimney when it was smoking. Close all doors and windows tightly to stop draught, throw a pound or two of common salt on the fire, wet a blanket and hold it in front of the fireplace to prevent the ascension of any draught at all. Fire can only live in the presence of air.

CHEST OF DRAWERS STUCK. How maddening when you have week-end guests! The most likely cause is damp. Put an electric fire near it and it will gradually shrink and dry out. Then rub the edges of the drawers and the runners on which they slide with a BB pencil. Thickly, so that the black lead makes a shiny surface.

CHINA CEMENT FOR EMERGENCY USE. For the restoration of some ornament, possibly the gift of a guest, now broken almost at the moment of their arrival. You have no glue or china cement. Is there still an egg in the house? Use plaster of Paris made into a runny paste with the white of the egg, press the broken bits together and lay them on the plate rack of the stove to dry out.

CHINTZ, TO CLEAN. Brush off the dust and wipe all over with a clean, slightly damp flannel. Rub in dry bran, well, several times, or rub until dry with a thick slice of very stale bread. It is not necessary to remove the chintz from its chair, only butter from the bread.

CISTERN DRIPPING. The ball valve is probably stuck. Turn off the water and see that it *is* off by pulling the plug. Take off the lid of the cistern and gently raise and lower the long metal 'arm' with the ball valve on its end. Frequently it gets stuck with a bit of grit in the water supply. If this is the case merely moving it is sufficient cure, you can turn on the water and watch the ball valve rising until the water reaches the line painted on inside of cistern and labelled 'water level'. This is one of those minor household miracles taken so much for granted and not appreciated until in abeyance. If ball does *not* halt at the halt sign, turn off again, undo with the pliers a little split-pin which connects the arm with the valve, remove arm and ball complete and bend the arm slightly downwards, which will, as you can see, make the ball touch the water sooner and receive the 'stop' signal quicker. It will no longer dribble. Replace split pin and arm and all will be well.

CLOTHES, TO DRY IN EMERGENCY. Suppose that something has been spilt on the only tablecloth adequate to the occasion and you have only a short time before putting it back on the table. Wash it through quickly, light the gas stove, all burners *and* oven, with oven door open and rig up an emergency clothes-line near it. The window must, of course, be open to allow the escape of steam. Finish off while still a little damp, with a very hot iron. This quick-drying arrangement is suitable for any kind of emergency laundry. But the window *must* be open. If dealing with small articles only an old umbrella makes a wonderful drier. Rip off the silk, screw a hook to the ceiling and hook the handle over it, peg the articles to the ribs. If it is not an emergency and you have time to do the thing properly paint ribs and umbrella to match your kitchen colour scheme. When not in use shut umbrella and keep with the brooms.

CLEANING CLOTHS, TO MAKE. The major disadvantage about polishing plate with liquid or powder is having to wash and dry it all afterwards to remove powder (or liquid) between prongs of forks or other lurking places. Prepare some polishing cloths and nothing else need be used. Boil some old cotton vests or similar garments in a saucepan of milk (new milk, cream and all) and hartshorn powder, one ounce to a pint—you can get it from any chemist. Boil five minutes, rinse in cold water and dry quickly in front of the fire. Plate rubbed with these rags never needs cleaning.

COLLAR WASHING, TO AVOID PEG MARKS. If you have

any *more* cotton vests, after the proceedings outlined in previous paragraph, sew some shirt buttons on one, all down the side at three-inch intervals. Button the collars on to these and peg the vest longways on the line.

COCONUT MATTING. Under the piercing inspection of your pre-party eye does it look a little jaundiced? It picks up dust no matter how often you vacuum it and you would like to wash it, but how to rinse it? Salt is a good bleacher and soda removes grease marks. Sling the thing out on to the lawn. On your knees (unless you can use someone else's) scrub it with a brush and a bucket of hot water containing a handful each of common salt and common washing soda. Then turn the hose on to it, sluice it well and heave on to the line to dry in the sun and wind.

CRACKS IN WALLS, TO FILL. Before distempering or painting it is best to use a 'filler' to make up cracks and chips and general wounds occasioned by chair backs and the corners of hard objects such as tables and beds. Ordinary plaster of Paris dries so quickly that in less than five minutes it is unmanageable and you are for ever running to the kitchen tap to mix up another lot. Instead of water use vinegar and you can mix enough to last you for the whole job. It will remain workable for about half an hour.

CRETONNE, TO WASH. Soap spoils the texture. Steep half a pound of bran in a little muslin bag as you do for a soft bath, and wash the material in this at a temperature, of not more than 100° F. Rinse in cold water and dry slowly away from sun or fire. Use a cool iron on the wrong side.

CRETONNE, TO MEND. Let us suppose that you have trodden on the frill of an easy chair five minutes before opening time or zero hour, just as you prefer. It is of no use crawling round and round the thing with a mouthful of pins and heart full of hope, trying to patch it up. The first guest will inevitably choose that chair and immediately rise with howls of anguish and laddered nylons. Cut a strip or two of elastoplast (according to the size of the tear) and stick them on the back at intervals of two or three inches, crossways over the slit to draw it together. Press them well to the material and they will last until the next time it is cleaned. Quite invisible. Which is more than you can say of a darn.

DECANTERS, TO CLEAN. A most common disaster is to find, when you want to decant the port, that a previous lot left tidemarks at intervals down the decanter and was not rinsed off. Crush some egg-shells, cram them through the neck, add half a pint of water and agitate them violently up and down and sideways. If no egg-shells, use rice, though this, being usually polished, is not so scratchy. Small pieces of coal used in the same way have also been known to be very efficacious and for very obstinate and crusty cases add a teaspoonful of muriatic acid to the water and leave as long as you can. If the stopper has stuck wrap with a cloth wrung out of hot water, then remove cloth and stick under the cold tap. It will shrink the stopper away from the neck. If decanter is very valuable and you fear the alternate application of heat and cold, run some salad oil round the stuck neck, put it near the fire, and when you think it has had time to work in, wrap a wooden hammer handle in a cloth and tap all round the stopper. It should come out quite easily.

DIAMONDS, TO CLEAN. Wash in your hands with warm water and Castille soap rubbed into a lather. Dry with clean blotting-paper screwed up into a point. This reaches into all the crevices and leaves them sparkling.

DISTEMPER, TO MIX. Use discretion with the water and don't be too boastful about how easily you can do it. Thin the paste with a very little warm water, muddled up with your hands, until there are no lumps at all and the consistency is that of cream. Slap a little on the wall and if it pulls it is too thick. If on the other hand it runs, it is too thin. Which is a pity, because you can add more water to thin it, but if you have to add more distemper to thicken it, it is difficult to mix quite smoothly again. Keep a bit of flat lath in the bucket to stir it pretty often and scrape out all the angles and walls of the bucket. Always distemper in a good light, preferably daylight, or you will miss patches. Tie a string across the bucket mouth from handle to handle and wipe your loaded brush across the string before applying to wall, to remove surplus distemper and save drips down the arm. For the same reason use your brush sideways with a flicking motion, rather than flatways, which spatters the stuff all over floor and distemperer. If two of you are sharing the job, mix all the distemper together and then divide it or it will be of a different consistency.

DUSTING AWKWARD CORNERS. Such places as picture rails and stair corners, the back of slatted chairs and beds and carving on those misguided museum pieces which our ancestors have bequeathed to us, are a vexation to the soul and a snare for homeless dust. The usual solution of a feather duster merely disturbs the accumulation for a moment. It all returns when things have had time to settle down again, and a vacuum cleaner, unless it can get closely up to the offending spot is not efficient. A common dish mop, soaked overnight in paraffin and then allowed to dry, will reach all awkward corners and the residue of paraffin absorbs the dust so that none of it flies.

ELECTRIC LIGHT FAILURE. Unless it's a power cut or a mere fuse, send for the electrician.

FEATHER PILLOWS AND EIDERDOWNS, TO WASH. Prepare some good hot soap-suds in a bath and swizzle a pillow about in them so that it gets well soaked. Squeeze it or run through the wringer with the rollers well apart and repeat washing. Do this once more and peg on the line to dry on a windy day. Do not hang in the sun or in front of a fire because extreme heat will remove the oil from the feathers. And do not be alarmed if the pillows look bedraggled, they may take several days to dry out and regain the proper fluffy consistency. With coloured eiderdowns it is wise to soak in a solution of salt and water (one handful to two gallons) to set the colour before having any dealings with hot water.

FEATHER PILLOWS, CUSHIONS OR EIDERDOWNS, TO REMAKE. Unless you take proper precautions getting any feather article into a new tick is worse than trying to cage an exaltation of larks. The whole house will be full of flying bits which you can't even attack with the vacuum cleaner, they are too volatile. The right way is to open one corner of the pillow or whatever it is and sew to it a similar opening in the new tick. It must be an opening about eight inches long, to give the feathers room to manoeuvre. Shake one into the other, helping the feathers through if necessary by a kind of 'milking' movement, unstitch them when the transfer is completed and stitch up the full one. You will find there is not a loose feather anywhere.

FIRE EXTINGUISHER, HOME MADE. Mix six pounds of common salt and three pounds of sal-ammoniac in two gallons of water. Pour it into large screw-top bottles, quart cider bottles will do if you have nothing larger, but empty petrol tins are better. See that they are airtight or the stuff will evaporate. See also that it is labelled clearly. It will not run a car.

FLIES, TO DISPEL. Flypapers are all very well, but at a party they will inevitably add to the hazards of entertaining by entangling themselves in the hair of guests. You will have to provide something less catching. Dip small pieces of sponge in boiling water and stand in egg-cups all round the room where not likely to be either seen or upset. Sprinkle on each half a teaspoonful of oil of lavender so that it gives off its pleasant scent for several hours. Flies dislike the smell intensely and will not go near it. To refresh this pleasant trap pour on a teaspoonful of boiling water about twice a day to start the oil evaporating again.

FLOWERS. You have all the information in Chapter 6. But if there is no room at all to put flowers and it is a summer party, do a nice arrangement on the window-sill, best side to the room, and leave the bottom half of the window open. If your view is negligible, non-existent or frankly hideous, why not make a permanent window garden facing inwards, admitting light through its sides and the top half of the window, but presenting, instead of the grisly view of roofs or walls or railway sidings, a little Japanese garden or miniature rockery with tiny roses blooming among dwarf plants and winding paths leading to small thatched summer-houses, or any arrangement that suits you. The making of miniature gardens is a fascinating pursuit and appeals to almost everyone, while making a fruitful topic of conversation, a very life-line with a shy guest. To be effective all the year round you need a kind of glass greenhouse built on the sill outside, just the size of the lower sash and provided with a roof to keep out the weather. It has glass sides and a glass front and any carpenter can make one in almost no time at all. What you have done, in effect, is to build a small conservatory on your window-sill, well strutted from below, where plants can grow in ideal conditions and out of draughts. Pile up some soil in one corner, sow grass seed, collect rocks and twigs and small seedlings of trees, and finally plant rose trees two inches high, with the dwarfest kind of rock plants, which will be a permanent source of delight. There is now a book dealing solely with the subject of 'sink-gardens', which your window garden will, in essence, be, and from the author one can obtain all the plants needed for this delicate delightful pastime, so that a hideous view is no longer a drawback, it is an excuse and a golden opportunity.

Food. Serve whatever you can from your own garden, no matter if the quality is not always outstanding. The flavour will be better and it makes something to talk about.

Frozen Water-Pipes. The best course, naturally, is to see that all pipes are lagged with felt, sacking, or even brown paper so that they *can't* freeze, and as an extra precaution, when frost is forecast, to turn off the stopcock and empty the pipes by turning on all taps and pulling the lavatory plug. But assuming that you have been caught napping, or can't find the stopcock (which is usually under the kitchen sink) and the pipes are frozen, it is frequently quite a quick and simple matter to un-freeze them if you know *where* to apply the heat. Have a look at your main cistern in the roof. It will mean climbing a ladder perhaps, but you should always have one of the right length handy in case of fire, and a bit of practice in shinning up it is not a bad thing now and again. The cistern, having been gazed at, will yield the following information. Water goes into it from the top. Water goes out of it from the bottom. There is a lead supply-pipe (on to which is fixed one of those ball-valve things we met in the lavatory tank) and at the permanent water level there is also an overflow pipe—the thing which drips on the tradesmen standing at the back door.

All or any of these may freeze, and the most likely point at which to find them stuck is their entry or exit to or from the cistern. You can't very well pour boiling water on them, except just where they are *over* the cistern, or you will drench the ceilings below, but I have evolved a handy un-freezer with a small toasting-fork and a yard of asbestos rope, bought for a penny from a garage. Wind the rope to and fro among the prongs of the fork and secure it from slipping with some thin wire. Take a box of matches, a bottle of methylated spirit and your un-freezer, mount the ladder and say good-bye to your family for half an hour or so. If you set the roof joists alight you will say good-bye to them for longer than that, so perhaps you had better take a flagon of fire-putter-outer, as described on page 61, or one of the party soda-water siphons, for squirting purposes. Settle yourself comfortably near the cistern, being careful to tread only on timbers and not on the intervening laths, which is bad for ceilings, pour a few teaspoonfuls of methylated on the fork and light it. Wave it to and fro under the pipes near the cistern, each of them in turn, and follow them along as far as you can. Repeat the methylated pouring as often as necessary, but not too much at one time. Sooner or later you will find the ice blockage and you will know *when* because there will be the immediate rushing of released waters. If these are rushing in wrong directions and there are cries of anguish from the scouts below, your pipe is already burst. Send for the plumber and go for a long long walk until things are better.

FUR, TO CLEAN. Make bran into a stiff paste with hot water. Smother the fur with this and don't panic. Rub it well in all over and shake out. Rub the fur dry with a woollen rag, old golf stockings are ideal. If you don't play golf or wear stockings use baby's vest. Scatter it with dry bran to absorb the last of the moisture and leave until next day, then shake out.

FURNITURE DUSTERS. Sprinkle paraffin all over a cloth and roll into a cylinder. Fit this into a cocoa tin and put on the lid until next day, when the paraffin will have permeated evenly all through the rag without being too damp in any one spot.

FURNITURE POLISH. Shred beeswax into a jar with a screw top. Add the same quantity of turpentine and the same of linseed oil and leave in a mild warmth until next day. Then shake until it becomes a smooth emulsion. A variation on this theme is to shred an ounce of beeswax (obtainable from any chemist) and half an ounce of Castile soap. Add half a pint of boiling water, half a pint of turpentine and two tablespoonfuls of methylated. Leave for forty-eight hours before using.

GAS ESCAPING. Do not look for it with a match. Make a paste of soap and water and brush over the pipe where the leak seems strongest. It will bubble if the leak is there and is not just a tap turned on accidentally. Smother the leak with soft soap and send for the gas fitter.

GAS COOKER GIVING A POOR FLAME. Remove the burner and prod the 'injector' where gas comes through, with a skewer or wire. It is probably full of porridge. Clean burner with wire brush and then scrub in water (hot) containing soap powder, ammonia and soda. If the flame goes up and down and at times staggers almost to extinction there is condensation in the lowest point of your supply. Gas goes under hot roads, then plunges into cold cellars, with the result that in summer condensation collects on the inside of the pipes and instead of a pipe full of gas, you have, at the lowest point, to which it naturally drops, a pipe half full of water. The gas fitter has an instrument especially for sucking this out, but if you examine your supply there is probably a little tap at the lowest point with a tiny nozzle. Turn off the main supply at the meter, hold a jam jar under this little tap, turn it on and you will probably be rewarded with several spoonfuls of water and a perfectly restored stream of gas on your cooker.

GREASE STAINS. Cover with French chalk quite thickly

and rub it in. Now cover with blotting-paper and run a warm iron over it. Repeat until grease is all absorbed. This is a good First Aid for any cloth and even for wallpaper. If it refuses to respond to this treatment more severe methods will be found under SPOTS ON THE WALL, page 73.

HANDS. Rub in a protective cream before doing any dirty work, or they won't be fit for a party, and as a routine precaution keep a jar of hand cream by the wash-basin and another by the sink. *Every* time you dry your hands, no matter how often this occurs, rub the cream well into them. But don't wear gloves for housework, they are too muffling, and a keen sense of touch, with an appreciation of fine surfaces, is one of the most precious human possessions.

HANGOVERS, HELP FOR. Half an hour before it is required of you to imbibe freely—and there are occasions where there is no option—drink a leisurely glass of good milk fairly warm and wash down two aspirins with it. Disaster comes not entirely by quantity, but by absorbtion into the stomach lining. If lining is coated with fatty milk, absorption is reduced to a minimum. A tablespoonful of olive oil has the same effect, but is less easy to lower. Assuming disaster already to have occurred, a good pick-me-up for next morning is Angostura bitters—a teaspoonful in half a tumbler of soda water. Equal parts of lemon juice and Worcester sauce with three large lumps of ice, in half a tumbler of soda, is very good too.

INTRODUCTIONS. The gentleman is always introduced to the lady, no matter what their respective rank. Give them a minute potted biography for a conversational lead, such

as that they both live in Minorca or Motherwell—play snap for high stakes—are interested in alligators or Picasso, or loathe music, and then let them alone to make the best of a bad job.

HOT ROOMS, TO COOL QUICKLY. If it is a summer party and the temperature seems to have risen unduly, dip blankets in water and allow them to hang in front of the windows for as long as you can before the guests arrive. They can be whisked away at the last moment. A bowl or bowls of ice on the window-sill will ensure that any air entering will be tinged with the flavour of the Arctic instead of the Infernal Regions.

MENDING A FROCK. If it is one of those nasty three-cornered tears in wool press it carefully down, joining the edges as neatly as possible, on to a strip of adhesive tape. If it is silk or nylon use Sellotape or some other transparent sealing tape. It is only a temporary repair but is quite invisible and turns a disaster into a joke. A frequent accident at summer parties is spilled tea on a white frock. Apply white shoe-cleaner and it is instantly cured.

NUT, IMMOVABLE. Soak with paraffin and leave for several hours. That is to get it *off* the bolt. To get it *on* when you can't make it catch the thread, turn it *anti*-clockwise until you feel it drop over a thread, then begin to turn in the right direction and it should grip properly.

ONIONS, TO REMOVE SMELL OF, FROM THE HANDS. If the effluvium seems persistent rub the hands with celery or parsley. To remove the smell of celery or parsley sprinkle the hands with a few drops of chlorophyll deodorant. If onion smell is on the air and the deodorant just mentioned can't cope with it, think seriously about having an extraction fan fitted in the kitchen window. They cost about £8 and whisk away the smell of all cooking without subjecting the cook to a draught.

PAINT, TO WASH. Begin at the bottom and work upwards. For some reason which I do not know, the water which runs down on to the *washed* wall does not leave a permanent mark, whereas if the washed part runs down on to the un-washed you may scrub until all's blue and it will always show.

PAINTING. Stir, and keep on stirring, the paint in the tin, until you are quite sure that it is all mixed to the same shade. Buy enough for the whole job in case there is a slight variation in colour, and if two people are sharing the work pour all the paint into one large utensil, mix thoroughly, then divide into two tins. Keep it stirred every now and then as you are working, but if you *have* let it get thick at the bottom, add about a tablespoonful of turpentine and a teaspoonful of linseed oil to thin it out. Use very little paint at each application and if there are cracks or uneven places in the wood, smooth into them a 'filler' such as Keenes Cement or plaster of Paris. It dries very quickly and must be sandpapered smooth before applying the next coat of paint. Be quite sure that one coat is dry before putting on another. Two undercoats of flat paint and one of gloss is usually right, and if you sandpaper it between each coat, it will look very much better. Never give more than one coat of gloss. It would not adhere properly to the one beneath it. Gloss on *flat* is the invariable rule. Remove spots, whether on windows or floors, before they dry, and rub those on clothing *at once* with a turpentiney rag.

PAPER-HANGING. Try putting the paste on the wall instead of the paper. It is much easier for amateurs.

PASTE FOR PAPER-HANGERS. Use plain flour, not self-raising, mix it to a paste with cold water, being careful to have no lumps, which will make bumps under the paper, then add boiling water with one hand while you stir with the other, until it is of the consistency of starch and as clear as gum. If it still looks like plain cold flour and water either your kettle wasn't boiling or you didn't add enough water. In either case the paper won't stick. You'd better put the mess into a saucepan over a low heat and cook and stir until it clears. If you want to keep it for any length of time add a few cloves before putting on the boiling water, and if you decide to call off the paper-hanging you can add some sugar and serve it as sauce.

PEARLS, TO CLEAN. Half fill a small tin with powdered magnesia, submerge the pearls in it, shake them about a bit and leave them overnight. They will be sparkling clean when you have brushed off the magnesia with a baby's hairbrush in the morning.

PIANO, TO CHERISH. Never mind about the temperature, the piano doesn't care. It's the damp that wrecks the tone. On the other hand too much heat and dryness will shrink the wood and be almost as harmful as too much moisture. If it is an instrument to which you are attached, and not just the one on which the children practise 'The Bluebells of Scotland' (in which case the dumber the better) it is worth while to buy a small humidity recorder and hang in the room. Failing this, regular and reasonable fires are a safe course, not a once-a-week bonfire half-way up the chimney.

RIBBON, TO CLEAN. And whether you believe it or not this is just as I have it from my grandmother. But they rather went in for ribbons in those days. Mix half a pint of gin, half a pound of honey, half a pound of soft soap and a tumbler of warm water together. Lay each length of ribbon on a cloth on the kitchen table and work this distinguished mixture into it with a toothbrush. Take up each piece of ribbon by both ends and dip in a basin of cold water but do not wring it, only run it between the fingers. Repeat with clean water and give it a third bath in another lot of water. Hang it up to drain until half dry, then iron inside a clean cloth. Finish off by ironing on the wrong side with a hot iron. If you have no ribbons substitute lemon juice for soft soap and bottle the mixture. It makes a very palatable cough cure.

RUGS SLIPPING. This is a very poor but very usual welcome to a guest. The family know all the slippery places and avoid them, visitors lack this specialized knowledge and it proves their downfall. You *never*, naturally, *polish* under rugs. But that is a purely negative precaution. Do you do anything *active* about it? Most cures can be found next to their diseases, and sure enough, as close together as nettle stings and docks, a non-slip felt for backing rugs can be bought from any rug-seller. But do not stitch it all round, that would trap the dust. Tack it at intervals of about a foot under the edges of rugs, and its special surface will suck on to the floor and stay put.

RUBBER RAINCOAT, TO MEND. Shred a piece of pure soft rubber eraser into an egg-cupful of naptha until it dissolves into a stiff paste. Paint on to each side of the slit at the back of the garment and leave a heavy weight, such as an iron, on it until it is dry next day.

SCORCH MARKS ON LINEN. You don't have to believe this. It smells too strongly of witchcraft. Nevertheless it is another of Grandmother's nostrums and it works, goodness knows *why*. If the linen becomes scorched by fire or ironing examine it to see whether the threads are actually destroyed or only discoloured. If the latter they can be perfectly restored by the following mixture. Mix half a pint of vinegar, two ounces of fuller's earth, one ounce of fowl's dung (from a cock if possible) half an ounce of soft soap and two large onions cut in small pieces. Boil this until the onions are soft and spread it thickly over the scorched place. Leave it until next day, then scrape off and wash the linen. It will not perfectly disappear at the first washing but will be paler each time and go at about the third wash.

SCRATCH MARKS ON FURNITURE. Drop some warm olive oil into the furrow and leave it until absorbed. The wood sucks it in and swells to fill up the scratch. Repeat several times, then polish with a stain polish.

SCREWS, USE OF. Dip a screw into oil before screwing into the wood; it will be twice as easy to drive and will never rust. If they have already rusted pour paraffin round the head and leave a few hours. This goes for all obstinate ironwork such as hinges and handles.

SCREW TOPS, STUCK. This is a particular failing of honey jars; the liquid honey is run in the jar at extraction time and solidifies, touching the screw cap. The same treatment as for glass decanter stoppers will unstick them—a dishcloth wrung out in boiling water several times applied to the cap, then cold water. This also unsticks fruit bottle stoppers whose metal rings have carelessly been left on.

SILVER, BLACKENED, TO RESTORE. Various things have an unfortunate effect on silver—egg, potato, salad dressing, coke fumes and so on. But the most obstinate stain yields very quickly to boiling in a solution of bicarbonate of soda—even salt stains of long standing disappear in about five minutes. There is now a proprietary liquid with the same effect.

SINK, STOPPED UP. Fill the hole with caustic soda and then pour hot water on. A 'ferret' should always be kept handy, a kind of long pipe-cleaner thing of flexible coiled wire which you can buy from any ironmonger. Screw it down for its whole length and then screw it back again and it will rid the pipe of any obstruction.

SINK BASKET. Buy three rubber suckers from an ironmonger and stick one on each corner to prevent it from scratching sink. Treat washing-up bowl the same way.

SMELLS IN THE KITCHEN. There are proprietary deodorants which will keep the air pure and delicate, but if by some mischance you have run out of these, try sprinkling lavender or coffee grounds on some slow-heating surface, such as the top of the boiler fire or cooker hot plate. It won't *remove* the other smell but it will cancel it out.

SOUP AT MIDNIGHT. This is a tactful hint that the party, so far as you are concerned, is over. Do not neglect to apply, or to act upon, this hint, according to whether you are giving or receiving the party.

SPOTS ON THE WALL. If these are of grease and you want to re-distemper that bit of wall you must first kill the grease. Wash if off with ammonia and hot water, then paint 'knotting' (from any builder) over the spot when the scrubbing is dry. If it isn't a very large spot and you have no knotting, colourless nail varnish will do. If these spots are on wallpaper you will need to patch it. You should have done it long ago. You have lived with that elegant swirl of brown spots since last turkey-time and never really *seen* it until you moved the chairs around to make a little more room. And there it is, unavoidable, unmovable and unforgettable, blazing at you like a new constellation from a winter sky. You can, of course, station some Faithful Friend in front of it with instructions not to move, and explanations to the others that his leg is stiff and he *cant* move. You can also hold the party in an hotel or import a palm tree as stand-in for Faithful Friend. But all-in-all a patch of matching paper is the easiest solution. There are usually some bits left by the decorators where they cut out a bit round the fireplace and the door. Think hard as to where you put these and then tear them up crazily into odd-sized, odd-edged portions. Smear their backs with a little paste and dab them on the spots. Don't use gum, it comes through. The irregular edges of paper make it quite inconspicuous and no one will ever know.

If the damage is of an ungreasy nature use crusts of stale

bread to rub it off, but do be sure, first, that no one has left any butter on them.

STAINS ON CLOTHING. If grease, put a layer of fuller's earth over the spot and press with a very hot iron. Repeat as often as necessary or rub with a cloth dipped in hot ammonia and water. Fruit or coffee stains on white clothes: first apply soap dipped in cold water, then paint (on the spot and nowhere else), chloride of soda, and immediately dip into cold water or the chloride will eat the material. For ink spots use chloride, and immediately pour hot water through the stuff into a basin, iron mould is treated with chloride and dipped at once into *cold* water.

STOCKINGS. Everything is ready and you go upstairs to change, then fall straight through your last pair of nylons, or perhaps *one* of it. You have other odd ones of the same texture, but none which match in colour. Throw any unladdered ones all together into a saucepan in cold water and boil as long as you can manage. Ten minutes will do if they are *almost* the same shade but if one is coffee colour and one ginger it will take half an hour. The point is that they *will* finish up the same shade if you give them a chance. Rinse them, squeeze gently and hang up by the heels. Get the hair drier blowing on them and I can promise you that in half an hour you can wear them. Try this on the hoard of odd and unladdered stockings that everybody's wardrobe holds and you will be surprised.

WASHING-UP. Never mind if you are too tired to do it after the guests have gone. But however tired you are I would suggest that at least you clear all the debris out of the sitting-room, open the windows, stand bowls of water

about the floor to absorb the smoky atmosphere, plump up the cushions and stack all the crockery in the sink. It isn't so much the actual washing-up that is loathsome, as the sight of the battlefield. It looks so terribly morning-afterish when viewed cold. Much better to give it a bit of First Aid the night before.

6

Doing the Flowers

As you know, every well-conducted house has flowers stuck about all over the place. And what is more they are DONE. They don't just happen, and it is part of the duty of every hostess, I feel, to learn the short cuts to this cunning art, so that in due course when she has to grapple with gladioli or display the delphiniums she can spare herself the acuter horrors of the battle.

There's no doubt that a few posies plonked down here and there are an enormous aid to entertaining.

They can form a botanical or aesthetic jumping-off ground for a conversation which would otherwise be a non-starter.

They are a convenient receptacle for things like olive stones, cocktail-sticks, cigarette-butts, exploded meringues and expended portions of paper games for which there is no other decent burial ground within sight.

They can be strategically so situated as to disguise shortcomings in the walls, scorch-marks on tables, or the unfaded portion of wallpaper where the family portraits used to hang.

They draw the eye away from less comely portions of the landscape and are a most exquisite medium for a bout of exhibitionism. If you really *want* to make your ego protrude all over the place and your aura obvious you have only to do a natty arrangement with cabbage leaves, artichokes, fir-cones and pumpkins and stick it on a small table with three legs, one of them if possible defective.

Everyone will fall flat on their face before it. Whether from admiration, or the fact that it's full in the fairway, or because of the dud leg one does not inquire. The effect is stunning either way and will set people talking like mad. It will get your party going with a bang.

Another use of flowers is to make a glorious great ostentation. Mrs Beeton, who knew all there was to know about entertaining and invented a lot more for herself, said 'Hostesses in the season vie with each other as to whose table shall be most elegant, and often spend almost as much on the flowers as upon the dinner itself.' Which means, carried to its logical conclusion, that if you order a plane load of orchids from Brazil you automatically outshine all opposition and there is no more to say about it.

If you aren't quite so opulent we'd better contrive a success with a few more common flowers and a sprig of this or that gleaned from the garden.

Unfortunately at the time of year when we give most parties flowers have practically vanished from the face of the earth, and weight for weight cost much the same as mink, but if you know how to arrange them quite a small amount will suffice. As with all other occupations, if you know what you are doing and why you are doing it the job is twice as quick and easy, and twice as successful.

Most of us can do a marvellous bowl of flowers. Sometimes.

At other times, with the same materials and the same utensils, it looks like a tatty collection of left-overs from the dustbin. And the more often it is torn to pieces and re-done the tattier and more tossed-together it looks. So that in the end, just before zero hour, we pitch the lot away, get down the pampas grass from the attic, run the Hoover over it, and have a good cry.

But if I pass on to you a few hints which put the thing on to a mathematical basis, so to speak, you can depend on a hundred per-cent success every time and no worry.

Everyone knows that the art of flower arrangement originally came from Japan where young ladies study it at college as ours study English. Only a great deal more profitably. I have even heard that a Japanese lady will sit for four hours on the floor steadily gazing at a branch of plum blossom and trying to decide which way to place it in a vase to best advantage. And certainly they have a special name for one of their most ardent occupations, which is *hana-mi*, or 'cherry blossom viewing'.

I don't suggest that you sit for four hours on the floor, but I *do* suggest that if we study our floral material and decide what is its line and style, then display it in such a way as to accentuate that line, it will double its beauty and usefulness and make the amount of flowers go much further.

Rule 1 is to decide on your outline (which sounds like the first lesson of a slimming course)—triangle, rectangle, crescent, fan, or whatever it may be—and place some foliage to indicate the line.

2. Fill in the outline with flowers, starting at the outside with small buds or flowers and working inwards and downwards with progressively larger ones. It is best to have three shapes of flowers, spiky, round and spreading. Embed this principle in your mind and you will always—in any material, even a bunch of twelve tulips—be able to find what you want. The tight tulip buds act as spikes; open out three flowers and turn back the petals to make the round shapes and the drooping leaves give the spreading effect.

3. Have a 'focal point' at the bottom—that is, something which draws the eye and acts as a magnet to hold the whole design together. It could be a big blossom, one opened up where all the rest are buds, one of a deeper colour, a bunch of carrots, or a patch of beetroot leaves, but place it *low,* where all the stems converge and it will accentuate the 'centre of gravity'. You can see already that the 'basic outline' of the Pampas grass has sagged almost to extinction, and it has unfortunately no focal point whatever. Not anywhere.

4. Don't put all your flowers upright, but let them flow out horizontally or in any direction that the design demands. In other words if they want to flop let them. They will anyway.

5. Never put two flowers level with each other, and let them dodge in and out of the outline to break up the hard edge. The days when we cut all stalks the same length and did them in the shape of a bowler hat (and if we were wildly artistic dabbed a few bits of gypsophila among them) have gone. We now cut the stalks all in different lengths so that no two shall be at the same level. Occasionally they break off afterwards which makes them *exceptionally* un-level.

6. Always choose flowers not for their size but for their interest and charm. The largest and loudest people are not always the nicest, and I would always rather gaze upon a twig with flowing curves and little gnarly boughs than a fine straight branch like a telephone pole. They are much easier to handle too. Think of a droop of weeping willow or a lupin on its second day indoors and you will see what I mean.

7. Adapt your design to your material and don't bully your material into accepting your line.

8. Use something other than vases as receptacles—urns, jugs, sauce boats, pudding dishes, pewter mugs, shallow baskets with tins inside, tobacco jars, silver cigarette-boxes (with a jar inside for small flowers and the lid half-shut on them), a pottery casserole, a teapot, any old thing that happens to be lying about and will hold water.

9. Stick to the bottom of this utensil by means of a dab of plasticine a thing called a 'pin-flower-holder' obtainable from any flower shop. The flower stalks are stabbed on to it and will remain in any position, wherever you place them. But don't let this holder be seen in the finished design,

RECTANGLE IN A PUDDING DISH 12 DAFFODILS WITH FOLIAGE

VERTICAL ARRANGEMENT 3 CHRYSANTHEMUMS · 5 IRIS LEAVES

SET HORIZONTAL BRANCHES SIDEWAYS ON PIN·HOLDER

CRESCENT OF PUSSY WILLOWS AND ANEMONES

"LAZY S" FOR A TALL VASE PAEONIES, ROSES OR CHRYSANTHEMUMS WITH BROOM FOLIAGE

PINK CHRYSANTHEMUMS · PAEONY FOLIAGE · PRIVET BERRIES PINK GLADIOLI · PURPLE AND PINK MICHAELMAS DAISIES

MASS ARRANGEMENT IN COPPER URN

cover it with a flower, a leaf or a heap of pebbles. Where stems are too thin or fragile to go on holder, wire two or three together and *then* try it.

10. Smash the ends of all tough stems with a hammer to let them absorb more water.

11. Put a teaspoonful of sugar and a charcoal tablet in the water and they will last longer. The floral art seems to be a hybrid between geometry, carpentry, botany, plumbing, doesn't it?

12. Varnish big bold leaves like laurel and rhododendron and they will look twice as effective.

13. Give the flowers a little new water every day but don't change all the water, it is too much of a shock to their system.

14. Don't stand them in a draught. There are more flowers killed by pneumonia than by either heat or cold.

15. See that the flower arrangement, *what*ever or *where*ever it may be, is stable. I have seen flowers which *fell* over by their own weight, *pulled* their container over because they were top heavy (with the big blooms at the apex instead of the base) or were *knocked* over because they protruded too far or in the wrong place.

It's all very well to turn the place into a conservatory but you must use a little discretion with it.

Usually pots of ivy (either growing or pretending to grow), hops in season and in reason, or some other inconspicuous climber is considered enough for the hall, with perhaps one fairly foolproof bowl or basket of flowers.

In a place where there is so much coming and going the

less the number of objects which one can break or spill, the better.

In the sitting-room use flowers that harmonize with your colour scheme if possible. If you are terribly colour-conscious make them harmonize with your frock as well.

And on a dining-table keep the decorations low. At a formal dinner they can be as impenetrable a barrier as you please—and the more of a jungle the merrier, from some formal dining that I have seen—all the better to hide behind.

Etiquette demands that you devote your attention to the guests on either side of you, and to cut off the view of what (either desirable or *un*desirable) lies beyond this cosy haven, makes it all the easier to concentrate. But at informal tables where conversation is general and quite likely to be a free-for-all, it is an advantage to see who is addressing you without needing a periscope to peer over the poly-bignoniums.

You can even arrange fruit centre-pieces, which serve the treble purpose of food, ornament and promoters of lively conversation, and you have only to look at some of the still-life masterpieces of the modern painters to see *how* lively it could be. On the other hand the old Dutch school demonstrates how richly ornate a collection of peonies, grapes, peaches, hops, vine leaves, beetroot leaves, roses and nasturtiums can appear—a feast for both eye and palate. It is positively pagan in its lush profusion.

At the other end of the scale minute boutonnières of the smallest possible flowers—well mixed—placed in cocktail glasses by the plate of every guest, with nothing but dishes down the centre of the table, is out-of-the-ordinary, out-of-the-way, and altogether delightful to contemplate.

As well as the Japanese arrangements mentioned earlier, which are definitely linear and conspicuously economical, there is the type of arrangement, popular in the Dutch flower pictures and lately revived with so much enthusiasm and ingenuity by American ladies, which is definitely massive and conspicuously lavish. There are few towns of any size or worth in America without a 'Garden Club' and the intent and intense study, amounting almost to ferocity, with which they pursue niceties of colour, harmony, balance, weight, containers, dried arrangements, packing materials to wedge the things to a hair's breadth in the proper position, preservation, combination and extemporization—is something terrific.

One of them assured me 'We go for this in a big way,' which was certainly no over-statement.

But basically the thing they go for is quite simple.

You have a container, preferably one on a stand, stalk, base, leg or plinth of some kind to give it added importance. Cram this utensil with common wire netting with two-inch mesh. A little is no use, fill the vase right down to the bottom and tight across from side to side, so that it comes just above the rim of the container. If container is conspicuously shallow, anchor the netting with florists' wire twisted through it, over the top, and tied round the base of the utensil.

Strip off the bottom leaves from your flowers because they will rot. Make a flat fan framework of flowers right across the container. Turn it half round and do the same again, thus dividing it into quarters, then place recessed groups of flowers in these bays. You can see that by doing it in 'quarters' the outline will be delightfully modulated, in and out, in and out, all round, which adds greatly to the interest instead of its being a smoothly domed pudding-basin kind of thing.

See that your colours graduate agreeably. Don't jump from yellow to red, for instance, without a bit of orange or amber to help the eye. And don't *dot* the flowers about singly like confetti. Make groups of the same colour and it will be like an artist's palette. After all, it *is* an artist's palette, and you are painting a picture, but you will find that it's a better picture if you keep kinds of colours together. And better still if you stand away from it, swooping and snooping and drooping, as an artist does, to criticize it when you think it's finished, and then doing a final fiddle or two to improve it.

But you will notice that colour is nearly always better, more effective, and more manageable, if you remove from each stem the green leaves which would merely dilute it, and use them, or others, only where you want them, not necessarily where they grow.

Condensed Hints on Flowers

Height of an arrangement should be roughly 1½ times the height of the vase—a little more if you like, but not less. Width is usually ⅔ the height.

When buying or cutting flowers, do it, if possible, at crack of dawn and stand them up to their necks in a bucket of water for several hours before arranging them.

Dry flowers for winter use by hanging them head downwards in a warm dark place—an airing cupboard is ideal. Hydrangeas, delphiniums, cornflowers, love-lies-bleeding, statice, cape-gooseberries and all the 'everlasting' flowers are ideal for this game. I have a friend who fills her pigsties and chicken houses with drying flowers all the summer and makes their normal occupants live outside. She even uses seed heads of cow-parsley, plantain, poppy and honesty, hemlock, nigella, iris, peonies, teazles, grasses, wild parsnip and thistle, and very beautiful they look.

Hydrangeas, if caught at their last breath, about September, cut off and put in very little water with a dessertspoonful of glycerine, will dry slowly and last all the winter, assuming the most unlikely and diverse colours from purple and red to green, according to how much acid is left in the plant at the time of picking.

Beech leaves must be picked just as they *begin* to turn yellow, because at that time they are still sucking up moisture and will absorb the glycerine into which you put them. If you wait until they're brown they have already relaxed their hold on life and ceased to suck anything. Stand in a jug of one part glycerine to two parts water after cracking the stems, leave them to drink for three weeks, and then spread them out under the carpet for people to walk on.

If no carpet put them under the mattress.

If no mattress buy them from a florist.

Water-lilies. If you want a delicious floating bowl for the dinner table you will be disappointed, because they close up at night. Drop a spoonful of warm-but-not-hot paraffin wax in the centre of each and it will keep them open.

Camellias, gardenias and magnolias need a tiny pinch of salt sprinkled in their middle to prevent them from turning brown.

Carnations like a pinch of bicarbonate of soda in the water.

Tulips must be rolled up in newspaper and steeped up to their necks in water, with about a teaspoonful of sugar to a pint of water.

Dahlias like their ends stood in boiling water for a few seconds and then plunged deep into cold water.

Poppies. Pick in the bud stage and burn the milky ends in a flame.

Lavender. Pick when the first flower is just opening.

Violets and primroses. Take up a small flowery plant, wash the soil off the roots and set them in a little crescent dish, one to each plate on the dinner table, with moss tucked round.

Forget-me-nots. Arrange low and read William McGonagall on the subject. It will cheer you up no end and the flowers will lead artfully up to a quotation or two. One has to keep this conversational hazard well in the forefront of the mind.

A wedge of McGonagall's Victorian verse declaimed at any dinner table should remove the last vestige of hauteur. Poetry is a wonderful un-freezer.

I *told* you flowers had more uses than one, didn't I?

Dried arrangements need no water, but if using dry material among living flowers protect it from the water in a small dry vase stuck among the wet stuff, or if dried pussy willow dab a bit of candle wax on the ends.

All woody stems should be scraped for several inches.
Nice colour combinations.
The first place always goes to blue-and-purple arrangements with a touch of either pink or lemon yellow. Try delphiniums with a 'focal point' of pickling-cabbage leaves and copper-beech substituted for their own foliage.

Purple poppies with grey leaves, blue cornflowers with dark purple prunus leaves, and pale lemon anthemis is good too.

Purple tulips, blue hyacinths and forget-me-nots, honesty and lemon or pink polyanthus is another winner, and don't forget to open out one or two tulips at the bottom by bending back their petals.

Pink arrangements need leaves of a pale young green or bronze. Try a spring thing of 'Fantasy', the parrot tulip, with pale lilac, pale mauve and pink aquilegias, and sweet peas, and foliage of new young beech or golden privet.

White peonies, leafless white lilac, rhubarb flowers and long sprays of white 'mock-orange' (leafless) mingled with grey and woolly leaves look wonderful in a pewter urn.

Crimson peonies look grand by themselves with their own foliage or with long sprays of laburnum in a large utensil. But keep it sparse and severe.

A July bowl of Dahlia 'Baby Royal', the pink keys of wild maple stripped of its leaves (if you live in the country near hedges), and young pink tips of pollard oak, mingled with 'Daily Mail' rose and wild yellow bedstraw, is a delicate symphony in a copper container.

Another spring decoration is mauve lilac, pink chestnut,

tamarisk flowers and 'Violet Queen' parrot tulips, with copper-beech leaves.

An autumn concoction of copper-leaved plum, berberis, creamy pink dahlias and traveller's joy is a beautiful sight.

A large basket for the entrance hall looks grand and imposing done in tall spires of rhubarb flower and pink peonies, and three long sprays of apple or cherry blossom in a blue jug convey instantly the idea of spring and blue skies.

While for a *dried arrangement* use bracken, beech leaves, cape gooseberries, yellow statice, iris seed pods and dried grasses.

One more suggestion will be enough. Use *green* flowers. Flowers of lime or oak in June stripped of their leaves and put in a copper or pewter urn are a revelation. Green hydrangea flowers, green hellebores, green rosebuds before they turn into white roses, green catkins, wild arums and passion flowers, the tall green spikes of foxgloves or greeny-grey of mullein, are wonderfully decorative especially if you take a bit of trouble and mingle them with green grapes, hops and decorative green gourds. Long woolly dangles of green love-lies-bleeding are beautiful with a spiky green cactus dahlia called Miss Rose Fletcher.

Why not grow some of these things, which are unusual and full of personality—ornamental kales and the coloured beets for instance, and when you walk keep your eyes open for a gnarly twig or a good-looking cedar-bough with or without cones. It will give a new point and interest to every expedition as well as originality to every arrangement in which you use it.

Flowers to Grow for Decoration

January and February. Dried flowers—honesty pods dyed lightly green and pink as well as the natural ones, seed pods, grasses and leaves.

Gather barley before the heads bend at harvest-time. Hang upside down until stiff and use it now. Very decorative and effective. Dock seed, dead brown laurel leaves, fir and cedar cones. Snowdrops, aconites, anemones and daffodils (forced), iris stylosa, crocus, iris reticulata, Christmas rose, winter heathers, winter jasmine, laurustinus. Pots and blooms of cyclamen, hyacinths, narcissus, tulips, freesias and coloured-leaved plants from the greenhouse.

March. Cineraria and primula in the greenhouse; catkins, wallflowers, polyanthus, hellebores, muscari, almond blossom, heathers, viburnums fragrans and Carlesii, and Mahonias Bealii and japonica.

April. This is the month when plants begin pushing up with what the French call 'abandon'. The English don't call it anything, they just oil the lawnmower and begin thinking about clout-casting with one eye on the sun and the other on the soil. You can gather cartloads of daffodils, narcissus, hyacinths, Lenten hellebores, alyssum, doronicum, anemones, and shrubs such as cydonia, berberis, daphne, crab and domesticated apple, cherry and kerria. Lilies of the valley are making a pale scented delight in the greenhouse.

May. Still plenty of tulips of a very decorative and colourful kind. Peonies (which come now in such wide range that they look like anything from water-lilies, roses and chinese lanterns, to balls of cut paper), bearded iris, lupins, phlox, anemones and ranunculis, sunbeam poppies, aquilegias, the first sweet peas, ceanothus and clematis, spiraea and mock orange, and a whole range of lilac from burgundy-red to the greenish-yellow of chartreuse. Dry pink or mauve astile and hang it up for winter use.

June. Iris, roses, delphiniums, sweet peas, peonies, pinks and carnations, gaillardias, calendulas, armeria and achillea. Wild clematis flowers and viburnum in the hedges. Don't forget to grow some of the dwarf belladonna delphiniums in both pink and a clear Cambridge blue. Artichoke *flowers* make a very smart and modern-looking arrangement when new; pull the petals apart, melt a candle and pour in the wax to hold petals apart. Hang up to dry and use in winter.

July. Still plenty of roses, sweet peas, clematis, sweet williams, catmint, antirrhinums, lythrum (a wonderful cyclamen colour), heleniums, and all annuals such as nigella, clarkia, godetia, larkspur, cosmea and clary.

August. The heat is thinning out some of the autumn-sown annuals but those you sowed in the spring are filling the gaps. Gladioli of every kind are plentiful and I advise you to grow as many as you have room for of the 'Primulinus' type. The ordinary kind are too heavy for anything but a large bowl, but the peach, orange and pastel shade 'prims' are a charming flower. Asters, zinneas, nasturtiums are abundant, with hydrangeas and ceanothus, hypericum and tamarisk in the shrub border.

September is for Michaelmas daisies, dahlias and out-of-door chrysanthemums. Anemone japonica and rudbeckia, golden rod and the first red leaves of vines and Virginian creepers, make 'doing the flowers' a matter of riotous colour-splashing, in bold blobs.

October. Still plenty of Michaelmas daisies and dahlias, the autumn crop of roses (which are usually better than the summer ones), berberis fruiting and turning colour, fruits of guelder rose and briony and misty trails of traveller's joy in the hedges, a shrub called Rhus cotinus or Wigtree with a bloom very much like a conical spire of traveller's joy, autumn leaves of every kind, plenty of autumn heathers,

kniphofias or red-hot pokers, zauchsneria and the last of the chrysanthemums. In the greenhouse (if you have managed things properly) there are chrysanthemums and carnations.

November. More chrysanthemums in the greenhouse and less outside. Plenty of berries and autumn leaves (grow spindle in the garden and sorbus aria, the white beam), yellow jasmine, winter honeysuckle, white snowberries (symphoricarpus), iris stylosa, a few early Christmas roses, and the first of the winter-blooming heathers. Use also tall spikes of dried dock. Pick it green, roll in newspaper, bend to the shape you want and it will dry in curves.

December. Your dried seeds and flowers will be working overtime. I hope you picked 'Chinese lanterns' before they turned orange, then snipped off the tips to make a green 'rose' with an orange centre. They are beautiful with beech leaves and barley. But there will be the first narcissus by now and cyclamen in the greenhouse, with the last of the chrysanthemums and in an open winter a good bunch of iris stylosa, Christmas roses, winter jasmine, polyanthuses and coloured willow or dogwood twigs pickable several times a week.

As for florist's flowers you can get anything, anytime, anywhere.

7

Some Ghastly Games

HAVING got the people to your party you must do something with them. Circulate a cocktail or two in a softening-up process, while you assess what form of entertainment is likely to go down best.

I don't mean that entertainment can safely be left to the inspiration of the moment. That is a ghastly fallacy productive of uneasy silences and a horrible hiatus between one gambol and the next, while everyone searches feverishly for pencil and paper and doesn't know what on earth to do with it when it's found.

No, I am an utter unbeliever in inspiration at crises like this—it is all perspiration, to avoid which you must have a list of games prepared beforehand, whence you can choose what seems appropriate to the moment, a proceeding which might seem to entail more work but actually means *less*, so that the hostess has an easy mind and can even, revolutionary as it may sound, enjoy herself at her own party. But make sure that you have the 'properties' needful to these frivolities all ready for action. I have known parties which needed soot, biscuits, a carving knife, two candlesticks and two night-dresses, a top hat, a pack of cards with each one cut into unequal halves, lipstick, a piece of coal, a walking-stick, a bowl of flour, 6 empty match-boxes and two empty beer-bottles. It is almost like

94

a treasure hunt before you ever start the party at all. But it is worth while.

Nothing is more macabre than a distracted hostess simulating a ghastly gaiety, with every game she ever played gone clean out of her head and a raging desire to burst into tears, take her shoes off, and be alone in the dark.

To avoid such mental anguish we will run through a few of the easier diversions and hope that something will fit your occasion. But if anyone shows signs of upsetting your programme by introducing a game of his own, *let him*. Don't dragoon them into being taught a lot of new things if they are bursting to leap into some ancient frivolity of their own.

Parties are like pigs. You can't *push* them, only *lead* them, and if it will run itself, so much the better for everyone.

It is always best to begin with a mixing-up game to get people acquainted and moving, rather than standing about shyly, and some highly successful ones of that kind now follow.

What about asking everyone to come bearing something representing the name of a town attached to their person. If you want to be choosy it can be a town 'in England', 'a town abroad', or whatever category you fancy, but by the time they have wandered round with a preliminary drink guessing each other's identities, or remained unguessed for fifteen minutes, no one will be shy and everyone will have spoken to everyone else on free and frivolous terms. Each guest should have a pencil and paper, and having guessed— but not disclosed— the town, should write it down with wearer's name opposite. There can be a small prize for

anyone successful in concealing their identity—and they will have earned it.

The secret town can be worn on any part of the body in any form. For instance, one of the most successful I know was a necklace of the tiniest possible brussels sprouts, culled from the very top of the stalk and no bigger than peas. They were threaded on green silk and appeared to be green beads. No one even *saw* them as a town, only a necklace, but there they were, in full view—Brussels.

A good variant on this was a lady with a cornelian necklace who had bored a hole in a small red tiddly-wink, suspended it like a medallion from the centre of the necklace and painted on it + E – B in gold. Everyone supposed that these were her initials until, unguessed, she disclosed that cornelians are pebbles and an extra E made it PEEBLES if you subtracted one B. The necklace idea caught on very well and next year one enterprising youngster in a green frock had tufted furry strands of fresh green moss on to green thread, stringing it in fronds like coral, and painted a cow in red on a gold milk-bottle top for a pendant. No one guessed that she was Moscow.

But the usual thing is to draw an object on a card and pin it to a lapel. For instance

Dundee—A large letter D painted in khaki.

Minehead is an early photo of wearer's head in a locket.

Holyhead—Angel's face with halo, painted on milk-bottle top.

Eastbourne—Picture of Chinese or Indian ladies or men.

Poole—Picture of a pond or paddling.

Or it may be an actual object.

Redcar is the smallest 'Dinky' car available, fastened to a safety-pin and painted red.

Cowes is two miniature animals suspended from a lapel pin.

Nuneaton is of course a whole biscuit, and either *Osborne* or *Nice,* one of that variety.

Runcorn is a drawing of wheat ears with legs (like matchstick men) running.

Wellington—(town in Somerset)—boot.

Mumbles—(village in Glamorgan)—head of old man and woman cut out of a cartoon and coloured; a balloon issues from her mouth, saying 'Speak a little louder, sir, I'm rather hard of hearing.' This could alternatively be Speke in Cheshire, or you can hedge and call it whichever one they don't guess.

Chard—(Somerset)—a piece of partly burnt wood or paper attached to lapel.

Bath—Tiny doll's bath as lapel ornament.

Banbury—A tiny banbury cake, home-made, worn as a pendant.

Eye—(Norfolk)—Glass eye from toy dog mounted as brooch.

Cannes is a miniature watering-can, and one can work out any number of others by looking at an Atlas index.

Prestonpans was another beauty—two dolls' patty pans

bored with holes and fixed on to a bracelet. On the base of each were stuck several words written on a bit of adhesive luggage label—'porridge', 'pansy', 'Wednesday', 'fly', and 'meter'. Anything would do; the point was that they were *pressed on pans.*

Towns and telegrams is another good un-freezer and only needs pieces of postcard prepared beforehand, one for each guest. Choose the names of towns with eight letters and write the first, third, fifth and seventh letters on one card and the second, fourth, sixth and eighth on another. Keep the odds in one bowl and the evens in another, giving odds to the ladies and evens to the men. The idea is to get them searching about for their other half which when combined makes a town. For instance R D I C and E D T H make Redditch, improbable as it appears at first sight, and so many of the evening papers run jumbled word puzzles that it isn't too difficult for the players.

Suitable towns are Paignton, Brighton, Hertford, Shalford, Rochdale, Saltburn, Grasmere, Greenock, Carlisle, Dewsbury, Abingdon, Bradford, Broxburn, Axminster, Cardigan, Wimborne, Clevedon, Falmouth, Minehead, Penzance, Portland, Llanelly, Radstock, Wallasey, Tiverton. And until you have seen it split up into odds and evens you have no idea what an improbable name Llanelly looks. But there is worse to come. Having found their partners the man takes each letter of the word and uses them as initial letters of an eight-word telegram.

Paignton for example might give 'Plutonium arriving in gun-carriage next time order nitroglycerine,' and the lady gaily does her share by reversing the wretched word and telegraphing back 'New ointment tried, no good. I am peeling.' But the selection of words should be tempered to the intelligence of the guests. The list here is fairly easy but just try making telegrams from towns like P W L L H E L I; in fact, if the two halves ever come together at all it will be a miracle. Even Penzance is quite something.

When everyone has finished—or a time-limit has expired—the hostess can read out the results, and if there was any constraint before there will be little afterwards.

They are now ready for a turn at *Orange passing*. Make two long lines, male and female alternately, and try to mingle the heights as wildly as possible. The leader of each team tucks an orange under his chin and it is passed down the line from one to the other with hands behind the back. Anyone who touches it, other than with the chin, is out, and if it is dropped that team begins all over again from the end. We usually play 'best of three' to decide who is the winning team and follow it with a sitting-down game like *Categories*.

Have about three papers for each guest prepared beforehand with six ruled columns across and six lines down. Choose any word of five letters and write each letter at the head of a column, leaving a space down the left side of the paper. In this space write (for example), on line one, Rivers, line two, Towns, line three, Mountains, line four, Artists, line five, Fruits—though the categories can be anything you like from kinds of aeroplanes to kinds of vegetables. If the word at the head, for instance, is P E A R S and the first row across, rivers, you could have Pamir, Exe, Arun, Rhine, Severn.

And if the next category is towns, it might be Perth, Everton, Aix-les-Bains, Rome and Singapore. You get the idea? Originality is a help here because they are read aloud in turn and you may score a possible ten for each line if ten are playing, and so on in proportion, but deduct one every time another player announces that he has the same word, so that you can see Llandrindod Wells would probably score over London and Helsingfors over Haslemere. The last time I played this, every person but one had Lemon for a fruit beginning with L, and the odd one had Loquat which made a good deal of difference to the marks. Add the score at the right of the paper and each person should keep his papers to add the totals in case you have decided to give a little prize.

About three doses of this one will be enough, it calls for a good deal of intelligence, and the next thing should be as brainless as possible—a card scramble perhaps.

The pack of cards which you cut into unequal portions should be *very* well mixed and then thrown in a heap on the floor at a given moment. Everyone drops on their knees and scraps wildly for *both* halves of as many cards as possible. You are not allowed to sit on, pocket, hold, swallow or otherwise capture any cards for the sole purpose of bamboozling your neighbour. Pick up half of, say, the Jack of Hearts, and having found his other half cast him to a safe place behind you, likewise repeat with anything else which comes handy. A spot of eye-gouging, pinching, hacking or strangling may be necessary before you can secure the second half of your choice, and is ignored by the referee, unless mortal. But to pick up a loose handful and park them under your frock while sorting the others is *verboten* and shows a nasty acquisitive nature. The winner is the survivor with the most paired halves.

Another good brainless gambol is *Matchbox passing*. It is the same as the orange game, but the empty shell of a matchbox is jammed on the nose of the leading man and he pushes it, hands behind back, on to the nose of the girl next to him. She prods it at No. 3 and so on, rules as for *Oranges*. The sight of an extremely tall man trying to manoeuvre a matchbox on to the nose of a very short lady without either embracing her or losing the box is a joyful spectacle.

A quiet one to follow this is *Memorizing objects* on a tray, prepared beforehand with about fifteen objects. It is exhibited to the company for any agreed time—usually thirty seconds—and then covered with a cloth. Each one must write a list of the objects. Variations of this is guessing the weight of collected objects, each of which may be taken up and felt. Ten is enough for this—list of weights must be written.

Smell testing is similar except that they take a good sniff at celery, salt, garlic salt, soap flakes, coffee grounds, nutmeg, cinnamon, tea, curry powder, cloves, carraway seed, thyme, sage, etc., all in small muslin bags. Pepper is barred and this and the preceding game are best played simultaneously, some guessing weights and some smells, then changing over. If it is a large party keep all three of the tray games going at once, and then have a noisy one to recover from the effort of concentration.

Really, *all* party games should be exuberant and a little noisy. If this is not your kind of caper you won't be playing games anyway—you'll be taking half-crowns off each other at bridge. But don't be afraid of joining in and looking foolish. Better be a duffer than a spoil-sport.

An *egg-and-spoon race* is a good noisy one. Give each runner a teaspoon to hold between his teeth with a ping-pong ball balanced on it. If a large party, they will have to divide into two groups. At the other end of the room is a row of cups, one to each player. At the starting signal they run to the cups, bend or kneel down, and drop the ping-pong ball in their own cup. If they lose it *en route*—if it

bounces—or if they don't get it into the cup, they must start all over again.

How-do-you-do is good fun too—for the onlookers, who must form two long lines, men on one side, girls on the other. The top man and bottom girl are blindfold and asked to walk to meet each other, shake hands, and say 'How d'you do.' No one must direct or assist them except to turn them back at the end of the row if they have by-passed each other. The players take it in turns until bored.

Did it ever occur to you that these blinded chasings and fumblings, grabbings and escapings, are a direct descendant of gladiatorial games? But I don't think *Feeding the Brute* has any gladiatorial ancestry, it is merely an infantile spectacle. Blindfold the girls and stand them several yards distant from their opposite man, into whose mouth each must feed one of those small chocolate beans called Smarties. Except to avoid being plugged in the eye, no man may move his head, and the chances are that a girl will not find her man or his mouth, or in feeding him she will drop the bait.

At children's parties we play this with jelly. You still can if you wish, but I warn you that it's death to carpets, and the one being fed from the dish of jelly needs to be enveloped in a sack with only his head poking through.

Which reminds me—an *Identity parade* with a large sheet covering one section of the room and half the players behind it is good fun. The sheet has a hole in the middle (I'm sorry about this but perhaps you have a punctured one), just big enough for each of the hidden ones in turn to poke his nose through. The other half of the company each has a numbered list and must correctly identify each nose, an extremely difficult proceeding, and then change places, en masse.

If you have a long room or are having a summer party out of doors, the range of games is enormously increased. An *ankle* race is run with each player gripping his or her left ankle with the left hand.

A *Jam-jar race.* Each player has two one-pound jars and uses them to walk on, moving one ahead and putting a foot on it, then balancing on that foot while he brings up the rear jar, places it in front and uses it to step on. Winner is the one who first gets from one chalk line to the other at opposite end of the room, without overbalancing or stepping on the ground.

A *Cork race* is a relay with men at one end and girls at the other. Number 1 man has an upright cork on the back of each hand and races to his opposite girl at the other end of the room. They exchange corks and she races back. Any spilled corks mean beginning again and the first pair to make an unspilled double journey wins. A *Needle-threading race* is similar—girls running with needles to men holding cotton; men threading needles and racing back, then sewing a button on a bit of cloth and running to the other end, then the girl picking an identical button out of a box, racing back to starting point and presenting it to the judge for inspection.

Indoor golf with a putter and a ping-pong ball which you must chip into a bucket is very good fun and there are hundreds of paper games, musical games, garden games, and card games. There are also intelligence tormentors such as:

Name as many things as you can beginning with the letter S in one minute. (Use any letter you like.)

Name as many animals (or birds or Christian names or anything you choose) beginning with the letter E.

Recite the second verse of the National Anthem.

What is the title of the *American* National Anthem?

Name the Archbishops of Canterbury and York.

Make a noise like a monkey.

Recite 'Sing a Song of Sixpence' multiplied by two (i.e. two Songs of a Shilling, two pocketfuls of rye, forty-eight blackbirds in two pies, etc.).

Recite a nursery rhyme, sneezing after every third word.

Say backwards any given proverb (for instance, 'a stitch in time saves nine', 'too many cooks spoil the broth', 'many hands make light work', or any other silly sentence).

Say the months alphabetically.

Say 'Shivering Sue threw the six fried fish through the shoe-shop sunblind' as quickly as you can.

Say 'I sniff shop snuff. *You* sniff shop snuff,' very quickly.

There are also the mass riots such as *Murder*, *Sardines*, *Treasure Hunts*, and *Charades*, which are actually *most* of them murder, but the most generally enjoyed, the most uproarious, and the one with the greatest scope for originality is *Copying a mime*.

A group of four people is sent out of the room and the host tells the remainder of the guests that he is going to act a wordless scene. It may be to catch, kill, pluck, prepare, cook and eat a chicken: or to bath a baby, prepare and give it a bottle and put it to bed: or a lady with a small dog goes to the butcher to buy a string of sausages, takes them home, cooks and eats them: or a lady with a basket boards a bus, can't find a seat, goes to a shop, buys a hat and goes home to show it to her husband. Or any other episodes you fancy.

The first of the four outcasts is called in and the organizer acts the scene as graphically as possible in mime and in silence. No. 2 is now called in and No. 1 acts it as well as he can to *him* but frequently without understanding what it is about. No. 3 comes in and is mystified by the antics of No. 2, and by the time No. 4 sees it and acts it back to the host it bears little resemblance to the original. Host now goes through his original actions for the benefit of No. 4 who is told what he was supposed to be doing. Another leader and another four now take the stage until everyone has had enough.

It is well to leave this fairly late in the proceedings, with one good romp—such as *Good Night, Grannie*—to finish up. For this, form two teams in parallel lines, one player behind the other. In front of the first man of each team is a chair bearing a nightgown, a child's bonnet, a pair of the largest possible Wellington boots, large cotton gloves, a candle and a box of matches. On the word 'Go' the front man of each line must don bonnet, boots, gown and gloves, light candle, dash round the line and up the middle again, blow out candle, leave it and clothing on the chair, and run to the far end of the line. No. 2 now goes through the torture, which is about equal for both sexes—if the men can't get into the nightgown, girls with small feet fall out of the boots. If you hurry, the candle goes out—if you don't, your rival in the other line finishes his circuit first. The bonnet strings will probably get stuck in a knot and the men will pull their jackets off with the nightdress or get stuck in it so that it refuses to come off at all. The first team to finish wins. But I am afraid the nightdress will be no more use.

You may think this is infantile.

Of course it is. But isn't that what parties are *for*? The more infantile the better, and I will guarantee that while any man is trying simultaneously to clothe his extremities in Wellingtons, large cotton gloves and a baby's bonnet while lighting a shaking candle, draping the fragments of a lady's night attire round his manly torso and hurrying madly to knock a couple of seconds off the rival's time, he won't be worrying about his work, his overdraft or his ulcers.

8

The Unexpected Guest

I AM by no means against guests. Only some are more difficult than others. And others, again, are the most difficult of all.

In this last category come the unexpected ones—those purveyors of panic and underminers of morale—who, because of your foolish, casually thrown-off invitation, 'Oh, do drop in and take pot luck with us. Absolutely *any* time,' now loom unescapable at the door.

Lunch-time also looms, equally unescapable, and as you compose your feelings sufficiently to answer the peremptory summons of the bell, you throw a hopeful glance at the sideboard, praying that she (or even *they*) may be on a milk-and-banana diet. But alas you have no bananas! The fruit dish is as empty as your mind, and you are utterly certain that the store cupboard is in the same state.

It doesn't matter that you've had the place full of the most exhibitionistic cookery for weeks—all teed-up and roaring for such an occasion which failed to materialize; the moment you are swept bare and not yet re-victualled will bring the casual visitor upon you.

One's natural instinct, when faced with this recurrent domestic crisis, is for flight. But there isn't a thing you can do about it. It's too late.

You advance with a smile so brittle that, one more fractional turn of the screw and it would crack right off, leaving your face as blank and empty as the larder and your mind, then you repeat the ghastly pleasantry about 'pot-luck', knowing that the pots are cold and bare and your luck right out.

But the resilience of the human soul is phenomenal. You no sooner extricate yourself graciously, having introduced her to the potted cacti and the current issue of *Vogue*, than you are extemporizing valiantly on a theme of six eggs, a tin of orange sections and a packet of brandy balls.

But *surely* you've got six eggs? Everybody has. They put them into waterglass for the winter and keep them in the refrigerator in the summer. It is not in nature for a household to be entirely eggless, and if I'm to get on with this chapter we will have to assume that they are there.

You will need four of them for an omelette for you and the Uninvited One, which leaves two over, and that spells soufflé. Decant your tin of oranges and make it up to a pint with orange squash or whatever liquid is handiest (even cider will do splendidly if it's the only thing you have). Heat a very little of the liquid and melt an ounce of gelatine in it, then pour it into a cold glass bowl and mix with the rest of the liquid and tinned fruit. Whip out the ice cubes from the refrigerator and immerse in the liquid while you lay the table and make bright conversation with the guest about the way the garden is (or is *not*) looking this year. By that time the liquid is all but set, and you must hurry to whip two of the whites and fold them gently into it before it becomes a rock. Pop it back in the frig. while you beat the four omelette eggs; add four tablespoonfuls of water, pepper and salt and a dash of herbs.

Your plates are heating in the rack, the gas flame high, and a knob of butter sizzling in the omelette pan. Pour in the beaten egg, let it crisp for a moment and then pull back the pan a little, so that only the half of it farthest away from the handle is over the flame, which you have slightly reduced. The egg on this half solidifies—pull it back over the other half with your fork or palette knife and let more raw egg run over—and so on until the whole runny mess is almost coagulated. Let it rest with the whole pan over the flame a moment to brown while you get plates and hot dish ready on a tray with the Ryvita, then fold it over and turn upside-down on the dish.

I say *upside down* where cookery books invariably say 'slide on to dish' because the portion of egg which first met the pan in its fine frenzy of boiling butter is the crispest and most lacy, and being at the handle end has remained untouched. The other half has been muddled about, and although it will be on top when the omelette is folded it never looks so good. Therefore turn it over.

And do remember that it will go on cooking for a moment or two after it is out of the pan, so remove it when it is *underdone*.

After the initial impact lower the heat or it will be tough and probably curdle. You can't hustle an egg without wrecking its constitution. And did you notice that I said 'add water', not *milk*. It is much lighter that way.

Of course if you have anything to put in the middle, such as a slice of ham, tongue, chicken or cooked vegetables (perhaps a bit of spinach, onions, young peas or mushrooms), it makes the omelette much more lively. But if you serve it quickly—crisply brown on the outside and runny inside—there's nothing much wrong with it in its simple state. And to serve a really perfect omelette is a way of wresting triumph and prestige from what looked like being a calamity. Reputations have been won and lost with less.

But we haven't finished yet.

You remember there were two egg yolks left after making the soufflé? When you bring out the empty omelette plates put a walnut of butter, a tablespoonful of sugar, two tablespoonfuls of cream and two teaspoonfuls of brandy into a small pan over a low flame. Drop the two yolks in and stir with a small wooden spoon until they heat and thicken—a matter of perhaps three minutes, but for heaven's sake don't hurry them, we're making a runny sauce not scrambled egg. Put a little silver sauce-boat on the plate-rack above, so that it's warm, then get the soufflé out of the refrigerator.

'And the brandy balls?' you very properly say.

Crack up a few on the breadboard with some heavy implement and scatter them on top of the soufflé. The combination of the soft spongy mass and hard crunchy trimmings is a nice touch and the same thing applies to the icy cold sweet and hot brandy sauce, but your total cooking time for the whole thing won't have exceeded ten minutes.

That's a menu for the larder which is really stark naked and down to its bare bones. Any kind of fruit will do—a tin of peaches, strawberries, oranges, grapefruit, anything you like, and in the very worst extremity you can make the same thing with a pint of orange squash and no fruit, or with fresh fruit.

If you haven't even the eggs I suggest giving it up as a

bad job and having a jolly little party at the nearest hotel. It's the coward's way out, but there are limits to what one should be called upon to suffer even in the sacred cause of hospitality.

If, on the other hand, you can raise even one small tin of something in the meat line, matters look much more rosy. You can concoct a beef rarebit with cunning ease, and it looks so much better than slices of cold corned

beef, although the ingredients are only the same. You can use corned beef, tinned steak, cubed luncheon meat or cold cut-up sausages (in a steadily descending scale); the principle is the same in each case. Tip into a saucepan the tin of whatever-it-is cut into inch cubes, plus a tin of tomatoes without their juice, or squashed fresh ones if you have them, pepper and salt and a dash of garlic salt.

If you *have* any tinned or bottled potatoes they go in with the meat. If you haven't you'll have to cut some fresh ones into quarter-inch slices, and cook them very quickly with the lid on in just enough water to cover.

While these are heating beat up an egg. Remove the lumps

of beef to a glass casserole that will go under the grill, thicken the gravy, boil up and pour over beef, strain potato slices, now softish but not broken, and place over the whole surface. Pour beaten egg over this and having grated cheese over everything stick it under the grill to brown while you are doing the table.

Simultaneously put a tin of peas in a pan to heat through, then strain them, add a knob of butter, a teaspoonful of sugar and a little dash of mint sauce, all shaken together, and there you are—if not a sumptuous repast at least a pretty creditable improvisation in a matter of ten minutes. If you have no egg we'll have to do without it and put a dab of butter on the potato slices to assist in frizzling them under the grill.

Curry is the same mixture, but toss in a few sultanas and some curry powder and, if you have time to do them, some peeled and quartered apples cut across once more into eighths. You can put pretty well anything into a curry and few people will have the courage to complain that it's unorthodox. I doubt if there *is* such a thing as an orthodox curry anyway.

You'd better cook the potatoes a little further than for the corned beef rarebit, then drain and mash them with an egg, to form a border for the mound of curry in the middle of the dish. But we must remain silent on the matter of rice, there is no way of cooking it instantaneously—though if you can spare a few minutes more you can do it in a pressure cooker. Put half an inch of boiling water in the bottom, stand it on a high flame, throw in a cupful of rice and a dash of salt, fasten the lid and give it ten minutes at full pressure before turning out the gas and raising the pressure valve to let out the steam. You can do your potatoes in the cooker at the same time.

For a sweet you can have omelette soufflé. Beat the yolks of two eggs with a tablespoonful of sugar and a pinch of salt (beating the whites separately) before taking in the first course. When you come out with the plates mix the yolks and whites carefully, get a knob of butter sizzling hot in the omelette pan and pour in the mixture. Don't stir it this time, let it cook from the bottom upwards, then put it under the grill to cook from the top downwards. Sprinkle with a few drops of liqueur, slide on to a hot dish and eat, if possible, with cream cheese. But it must *really* be cream cheese, the kind one makes when the milk goes sour, not those rubbery atrocities, tinfoil wrapped, which one buys in boxes from the grocer.

Another simple variation on the corned beef theme is fritters—which are merely thickish slices dipped into beaten egg and breadcrumbs and fried in butter. Tinned ham done this way is grand, good enough to serve even when there *isn't* any emergency.

For corned beef hash, a dish much loved by Americans, you need mashed potatoes. Granted the existence of these despised and indispensable vegetables, you mingle the beef and potatoes in any desired proportions, sprinkle with pepper and cook into one mighty pancake in a greased frying-pan. Brown the top under the grill. Make a couple of dents in it and fill with poached eggs.

If you have *no* potato, just break up the beef and mix it with beaten egg, then pancake it—or cut into slices on a fireproof dish, arrange a ring of tomato or onion, on each piece and brown under the grill.

Another diversion is *rissoles*, for which you break up the meat finely—melt a knob of butter in a saucepan, add two tablespoonfuls of flour, a cup of milk and a teaspoonful of Bovril and cook until thick. Add the meat and some pepper, with garlic salt if you like it. Turn out on to a floured board, make into 'sausages', roll in beaten egg and breadcrumbs and fry.

If the guest shows the slightest symptom of making a day of it the odds are that you have nothing for tea either. It always happens like that so you'd better leave a few extra potatoes cooking while you have lunch and think what you can do with them.

We will suppose the worst and assume you haven't any bread, though I think that, in this case, you must be the world's most improvident housekeeper. Mash up the potatoes while still hot and add to them two ounces of melted butter, a little milk and salt, and just enough flour worked gradually into them to induce them to hold together. It usually works out at about three level tablespoonfuls of flour to half a pound of potatoes. Roll out, cut into circles and at tea-time cook in a frying-pan or on a hot plate.

Baking-powder rolls are dead easy too. Put the oven on as for pastry, then take a pound of self-raising flour, add another two teaspoonfuls of baking powder, half a teaspoonful of salt and enough milk to make soft but not sloppy. Break off egg-sized pieces, mould very slightly and quickly into balls, and put on a greased tin. Brush with egg and milk and cook fifteen minutes. They are much nicer than baker's bread and the famous Irish soda bread is pretty similar.

It takes 1 lb. plain flour, 1 teaspoonful salt, 1 tablespoonful sugar, 2 teaspoonfuls cream of tartar and 1 teaspoonful bicarbonate of soda with half-pint (or less) of milk—sour if you have it, but with a teaspoonful of vinegar in it if you haven't.

Half and half white and wholemeal flour makes a beautiful moist wholemeal bread. Mix it very quickly, form into two flat cakes, and bake fifteen minutes at 375°F.

There are all kinds of small unscrupulous tricks like that which you can play when there's nothing to eat and no time to make it in, and they are usually such a roaring success that you gain a quite undeserved reputation as a good cook at the same time. Girdle cakes for instance: 4 tablespoonfuls S.R. flour, 1 egg, 1 teaspoonful of sugar, 1 of baking powder and a pinch of salt with just enough milk to make a stiff spongy dough. *Hurry* and cook it in spoonfuls (about 7 to a pan) before the baking powder all fizzles out of it. Turn them when brown underneath.

You can even make six-minute scones, with 8 oz. of S.R. flour, a good teaspoonful each of baking powder and sugar, 2 oz. butter, a scatter of sultanas, a little sour milk and a frying-pan.

You haven't any sour milk? Well then use the other sort and a spoonful of vinegar as we did before. Grate butter into flour with the cheese-grater for quickness, add the other ingredients and enough milk to make a soft dough. Grease and heat the pan, throw in your lump of dough, pat it out to fit the pan and let it cook half-way through. When brown and cooked on the bottom loosen it and toss like a pancake.

I can't help it, you'll just have to practise. We're in a hurry, aren't we? If you want to do the thing the usual way, rolling out on a floured board, stamping and cutting and fiddling about, you are leaving your guest unattended and we're trying to avoid this. Total cooking time my way is about three minutes a side if you haven't made it too thick. You can't even get the tea-things on the tray in the time.

When it's done pop it on a plate, cut it into wedges and let everyone split and butter for themselves. It's another reputation-maker.

With any of these emergency measures requiring egg— such as girdle cakes—a pretty similar effect is obtained with custard powder when you have sunk so low that you can't even produce an egg, and I once made a batch of these by using semolina, custard powder, quaker oats and ground almonds. They were voted first-class, but that may only have been politeness. The sugar was the genuine article but all else were substitutes. Or even substitutes *for* substitutes.

For a cake substitute on one of these grim occasions you'd better try oatmeal biscuits: ¼ lb. flour, ¼ lb. rolled oats, 2 oz. sugar, 2 oz. butter, 2 oz. coconut, a dessertspoonful of golden syrup and a level teaspoonful of bicarbonate, with enough warm milk to make a stiff dough. Mix the dry ingredients, rub in the butter, add treacle and milk, and roll out ¼ inch thick. Cut into diamonds and bake on a greased tin at 350°F for fifteen minutes. Let them cool slightly before moving off the tin.

Coconut pyramids are another winner and so simple that they come in the 'school-girl cookery' class. Of course if you *haven't* any coconut you can't make them but you've got to have *something* in the food store surely. You can't be out of everything.

Just put the coconut in a bowl when you've found it and add as much sweetened condensed milk as it will take without being either too sticky or too crumbly. Form into small cones by pressing together with the fingertips and put in a moderate oven for a few minutes just to crisp the outsides. Don't let them brown more than a mere  fraction. Five minutes will do if the oven is right. Leave them to cool a bit before lifting. It is possible to use almost any kind of cereal in the same way—for example puffed wheat or rice, crumbled shredded wheat and rice crispies, mixed with the condensed milk and dumped in tiny heaps on a greased tin. It's not good cookery but it's a face-saver and a time-saver and that's what we're after.

Let us suppose that you want to make scrambled eggs for two with one egg. I can't think why you *should* but you just *might*. Add a tablespoonful each of fine white breadcrumbs and top-of-the-milk with an ounce of butter and you may escape undetected.

I have even served up yesterday's ham sandwiches as a luncheon dish by dipping into beaten egg and breadcrumbs and then frying. Actually they are rather a toothsome morsel if there are plenty of them. Similarly jam sandwiches, date-lemon-and-honey, or banana-and-walnut, can be dipped in egg and milk, then laid in a shallow fireproof dish with the rest of the egg and milk (sweetened and flavoured with vanilla) poured over them. Put under the grill (with the flame adjusted fairly low) when you take in the first course and they will be a highly ingenious form of bread-and-butter pudding when you are ready for it. Or if the oven is already hot bake them and they'll be even better.

But the prize for grim, down-to-bedrock catering goes to my daughter, who, on an occasion of dire necessity and utter barrenness, mixed a little mashed potato, some porridge, chopped stewed prunes, custard powder, stale cake crumbs and sugar into a kind of spiky dough. She then dumped it in small heaps topped with cornflakes on a greased tin, and baked it for a quarter of an hour into a very creditable, if mysterious, kind of rock cakes.

I recollect that the only other thing in the larder (it was war-time) was a bag of dried peas and some curry powder, both of which she fortunately overlooked.

But it is too depressing to continue talking about empty larders. In real life there very rarely *is* such a thing and I can't imagine any hostess, however reluctant, being without the odd tin of lobster, sausages, herrings, salmon, steak, mixed vegetables, ham or fruit. Not *all* of them perhaps, though I can't think why not, but certainly some of them. It will make a great difference to our morale if we may suppose that you have just the most elementary hoard of this kind. They're not very exciting I admit, but it's what you do with them afterwards that counts.

For instance *pear meringue* made by setting the drained halves from a tin of pears on small rafts of sponge cake, covering with meringue and baking ten minutes to crisp it. If you've forgotten how to make meringue (and it's surprising how even the most elementary principles of cookery desert us in a crisis), take 2 oz. of castor sugar for every egg white.

Whisk the white stuff. Whisk in a teaspoonful of sugar. *Fold* in gently about three-quarters of the sugar, use the meringue and sprinkle more sugar on top.

Serve with the yolk made into a thin sauce with brandy, top-of-the-milk, butter and cornflour, sweetened and kept hot until the last minute. It is a change from the chocolate sauce which is so inevitably teamed with pears.

You can have all kinds of fun with a tin of lobster. Broken up, flavoured highly with pepper and a dash of anchovy, mixed with white sauce, lemon juice, and chopped parsley; put into a shallow fireproof dish, sprinkled with brown breadcrumbs and dotted with butter, it becomes a *lobster pie* when it has had ten minutes under the grill. Time to make—including the sauce—is five minutes, and you can use *haddock* or any cooked fish to delicious advantage in the same way.

Lobster cutlets are made in exactly the same way as corned beef rissoles if for 'Bovril' you read 'anchovy sauce' and put a bit of uncooked macaroni in the thin end for an imitation bone when you shape them.

It is a grim thought that in this 'empty larder' session even the bones are substitutes and hollow imitations.

Herring pie is a tin of herrings or pilchards with that rather anonymous kind of liquid poured off, the fish laid in a shallow fireproof dish, sprinkled with pepper and lemon juice, and a beaten egg poured over. It makes a kind of quick fish toad-in-the-hole. And a tin of sausages laid in a baking-dish and covered with two tablespoonfuls of flour, an egg, and half a pint of milk, well whisked while the oven is heating, makes a sausage toad in the hole.

Put your pan on the top shelf to heat as soon as you turn

the oven (full) on, then it will be hot and frizzle the edges of the batter nicely as it is poured in. Give it twenty minutes on the top shelf at meat-roasting heat.

Bacon rolls are a slice of bacon rolled round a teaspoonful of tinned steak, secured with a cocktail-stick, dipped in egg and breadcrumbs and fried in deep fat for two or three minutes. They look (and taste) very good sitting on a base of tinned spinach.

The foregoing is impromptu entertaining at starvation level, but every sane housewife has a selection of stored ingredients, and with a bit more liveliness and ingenuity in the selecting you can have as wide a variety of dishes for the Unexpected Guest as for the long-planned party.

Everyone likes apple crumble for a sweet.

If you keep the topping (6 oz. Demerara sugar, 3 oz. butter, 6 oz. flour) mixed in a jar, it is the work of a moment to open a jar of your home-made apple purée—or bottled black currants, gooseberries or plums drained of their juice—pack the topping over them and bake for half an hour at 325°F. You will have to keep the conversation going a little longer than with some of the other dishes, but it's worth while, and if you serve a soup and a meat dish you can do it handsomely.

To follow another meal *gooseberry fool* served in goblets is a change, and is merely some left-over custard out of the frigidaire mixed with puréed gooseberries and flavoured with sherry. You will undoubtedly have one of those cellophane-wrapped packages of sponge cakes stored in a tin with your shortbread (either of these keep for months). Cut the sponge cakes in half longways to make fingers and serve with the fool, or use chocolate finger biscuits.

And with a stored jar of lemon curd and a flan case out of a tin you can make a *lemon meringue pie* in a few minutes which will cook while you are toying with the first course. Any kind of pastry will keep in an airtight tin for weeks, ready to be filled and re-heated in an emergency. *Vol-au-vent* cases can be filled with lobster, crab, ham, haddock, chicken or corned beef mixed with sauce and heated for a main dish; or if it's a sweet you're short of, fill the case with tinned plums, peaches, pears or apricots mixed with custard and warm in the oven to crisp it.

Keep your oddments of flaky pastry in the same tin as the flans. Trim them to equal sizes, spread the bottom one with jam and lay another on top, spread that with cold custard and top with a third. Pour over this hot icing, which is two tablespoonfuls of your stored fondant melted in a saucepan, and scatter with grated chocolate. It sets at once.

Cut it into fingers. But do remember to use the sabre-toothed bread knife to cut it with, and go gently, or it will instantly squeeze out its custard and probably skid on to the floor. If it fails to do this you have made *Mille feuille slices* without knowing it. You can even make them (having no custard) with one layer of jam and one of apple sauce and still look your guests in the eye. They won't know that you didn't *intend* to fix it that way. There has actually been on the market for years a commercial puff pastry in 1 lb. blocks which will keep in the refrigerator for weeks and be worth its weight in gold combined with mincemeat, jam, fruit, steak or any other kind of pie or tart which you may be concocting for the sudden guest. But use them one at a time, you understand.

The finest and most spectacular face-saver of all (if you are not entirely out of touch with civilization) is a *soufflé en surprise*. If guests have applauded your clear soup (which was only Bovril and boiling water with a tin of diced mixed vegetables) and acclaimed the *vol-au-vent* of corned beef, they will fall flat on their face before the soufflé because it is one of those cunning conjuring tricks so exquisitely easy and so apparently impossible.

We will suppose that The Worst Has Happened and the Unexpected Guest arrived.

Is there a messenger in the house?

Then send them to the nearest purveyor of ice-cream for a good hard brick.

Meanwhile put a layer of your stored sponge-cakes (two cut in half horizontally to make four, for four people) on two layers of white kitchen paper on a small chopping-board, a sort of House that Jack Built, and switch the oven to 450°F. Put jam on the sponge cakes and when panting messenger arrives with brick put it on sponge (the brick I mean). Sponge should be an inch larger all round than the brick. Beat up three egg whites until stiff, beat in a teaspoonful of castor sugar, then sift in two spoonfuls lightly. Spread thickly *all over* ice brick and sponge, not leaving a piece uncovered anywhere, and sift another 2 oz. of castor sugar thoroughly over all. Pop in oven and take the meat course into the dining-room.

By the time it is finished so will the soufflé be. The meringue will be crisped all over and the ice still as cold and hard as a glacier. If anyone complains that the combination cracks dentine off teeth you can assure them that it's well worth it. In any case it is untrue.

It will look like a million dollars and taste like a miracle but I do assure you that it's a thing any child could make. It is again an example of legerdemain. That quickness of the hand which deceives the eye is the real secret of keeping the ice cold and the rest boiling hot.

A hot chocolate sauce goes well with it, and if you are wise, every time you make custard, white sauce, mayonnaise, bread sauce, mustard sauce, caramel sauce or chocolate sauce you will make twice as much as you need and put the rest in the refrigerator for warming up. If no one comes the family can use it next time, so it's a labour-saver in any case.

That covers about all the necessary ground, I think.

But you can see that to fill up the store cupboard is going to remove a lot of worry from you and make you a much less reluctant hostess. You can do the self-filling-up on days of comparative leisure and vary the contents according to your personal ideas.

I assume that you already have all the harmless routine things like sardines and ham, tinned oysters, lobster, salmon, prawns, pineapples, paté and palm hearts. But if you can become a bit more adventurous and bottle, in a pressure cooker, vegetables, meat, soups, and even mixed things like curries and risottos, you will have the repertoire of a Cordon Bleu and a million friends. Here is a list of the extras you can make for yourself and which will obliterate all terrors of impromptu entertaining. But be sure to do meat and vegetables with a pressure cooker. The ordinary oven-bottling method doesn't sterilize them sufficiently.

Things to keep in the Store Cupboard

Bottled. Peas, celery hearts, tomatoes, potatoes, asparagus, seakale, carrots, beetroot, parsnips, green and broad beans, chicken meat, risotto and any fruit including strawberries.

Puréed in bottles. Apple, tomatoes, gooseberries, parsnips, loganberries, apricots.

Soup in screw-top bottles. Meat, pea and lentil.

In small jars. Grated cheese, buttered crumbs, garlic salt, celery salt, home-grown herbs, mint sauce, horseradish sauce, dry breadcrumbs for fish.

In 1-lb. jars. Curried chutney mixture ready for use, fondant for icing, crumble mixture for crumb pies, lemon curd, grated chocolate, castor sugar with 2 vanilla pods in it to flavour the sugar.

In tins. Flan cases, *vol-au-vent* cases, meringues and small tartlet cases, large sherry cake, sponge cake for trifle, etc., sponge ring to fill with ice-cream and fruit, but keep pastry in one tin and cake in another. It stands to reason that you can't keep some things moist and other things crisp in the same tin.

In refrigerator. Cold custard and sauces, scalded evaporated milk. Thin large pancakes rolled in wax paper and packed into the plastic box of the frig. Spread them with raspberry or apricot jam, cut in half, dip in egg and biscuit crumbs and fry. You don't need to stand watching them as you do ordinary pancakes and they're much more of a 'party sweet'.

In a bucket of waterglass. Eggs and more eggs and then a whole lot more.

With a store cupboard like this you can, at a moment's notice, concoct such dazzling lunches as:

Cream of tomato soup
Sauté chicken breasts with mush-
    rooms, peas and new potatoes
Soufflé en surprise

★   ★   ★

Cream of chicken soup
Asparagus or mushroom omelette
Apple crumble

★   ★   ★

Clear Julienne soup
Beef rarebit
Lemon meringue pie

★   ★   ★

And who could want better than that?

Postscript

ADMITTEDLY entertaining entails work, but if it's a life of unrelieved sloth you're after, you'll bore yourself and everyone else to death and kill off all your friendships at such a rate that there will be no *need* to entertain.

And never suppose that because your means are limited parties are ruled out. If people have less money than formerly they also (fortunately) expect less in the way of elaborate entertaining, and it is better to put on a simple, informal party with pleasure and confidence than a banquet with care and apprehension. They were only a worry, both in prospect and retrospect and all too apt to develop into a competition in ostentation.

Let's forget to be grand and be jolly instead.

Entertaining isn't just ordering a gargantuan meal and then writing a proportionate cheque. It is planning the most pleasure for the most people with the least pain to yourself.

It means checking over the domestic machine beforehand to see that the wheels are turning smoothly; snipping off the flower stamens if you have a guest who is allergic to pollen; remembering who likes China tea and who Indian; throwing the greatest bores together so that they cancel each other out; ensuring that the drinks are cold and the towels hot; making certain that the laundry has come home and that no cooking smells escape from the kitchen; that there are ample cigarettes and matches and that you have rehearsed the cooking operations so that there are no hitches in your time-table—no horrible hiatus while you make valiant conversation and pray for the instant incineration of a pallid roast.

In fact, party giving is attention to the *little* things rather than the *great*—taking infinite pains for the comfort of your guests, and thus ensuring that your mind is placid and tidy and you have the leisure and the confidence to enjoy your own party. Nothing kills joy so quickly as a careworn and haggard hostess.

However, there's no *need* to be careworn. Entertaining is really tremendous fun, but you need to jump into the thing with both feet if you are to get the best out of it. Like everything else, if done half-heartedly it is a pain in the neck, a bore and a nuisance. You can't dodge it, so you'd better immerse yourself thoroughly and go for it in a big way. Your reward will be your feeling of achievement and the admiration of your friends.

So let us eat, drink, and be merry, for tomorrow——
But we will leave tomorrow to speak for itself.